THE TRUSTED
TRAINER

THE TRUSTED
TRAINER

HOW TO ATTRACT, AMAZE AND KEEP YOUR PERSONAL TRAINING CLIENTS FOR LIFE

DAVID OSGATHORP

WHAT OTHERS ARE SAYING

MICHELLE COLLINS
ACTRESS

I've worked with David for nearly ten years. He's my secret weapon when I need to prepare physically for a role. My life can be very hectic but David understands this and his thoughtful and considered approach gives me a calmness and focus to deal with everything. He's also become a good friend and someone that I can really depend upon, but his book won't be as good as mine!

JEFF SALMON
BUSINESSMAN AND TV PERSONALITY

I have worked with a number of trainers over the years but none of them have given me the knowledge, understanding, care and, perhaps most importantly for me, FUN, that I have working with David. I have a very hectic life but my sessions with David have become an importantly integral part of my week, calming me down and stretching the stress out of my oldish body. And unusually for an ol' grump like me (who tries to keep himself to himself) we have built a great friendship during this time.

CLAUDIA MILNE
TV JOURNALIST AND LONG-TERM CLIENT

David has been fantastic at looking after me. He's a very intelligent and hard-working young man and I not only enjoy the creative training sessions he gives me, but also some lively conversations about current affairs and a sick sense of humour that we certainly share. He has more ideas than he knows what to do with and is very stubborn – I think he's only written his book because I told him he couldn't do it! Good on you, David.

JACK BENTATA
BUSINESSMAN AND CLIENT FOR OVER 10 YEARS

I have known David for nearly 14 years. I am sure that he wished to open his own enterprise not merely for financial reasons but much more to enable him to be unshackled, giving him that essence of life, freedom to develop his rich ability to communicate and express and understand each client's individual needs.

Over the years David has built up a team of like-minded physical training experts, teaching them the philosophy of personal training for exercise, fitness, diet and wellbeing. Life is a journey and David is continually seeking ways – sometimes even the smallest detail – to enhance the service which All About You provides.

Those of us fortunate enough be part of his clientele are benefitting from increased fitness, feeling better mentally and physically and a wonderful experience at each visit.

RICHARD HUNTER
EXECUTIVE HEAD TEACHER AND CLIENT FOR OVER 10 YEARS

The trust and respect between a client and their Personal Trainer is crucial if it is to make a long term and sustainable difference. As a busy mature professional, I need a trainer who understands the fitness needs of my lifestyle, has the ability to offer challenge and knows exactly how far to push me. This awareness of my personal and physical capacity creates a unique level of trust and enables me to enjoy each session and believe that anything is possible. I feel fortunate to have found David, who combines excellent knowledge of fitness and training with excellent personal qualities – the perfect combination which ensures that the client-trainer partnership will last.

ACKNOWLEDGEMENTS

To the guy who said I couldn't,
And the one who said I shouldn't,
To the team that made it work,
To the times I went berserk.
To my old mate Stevie G,
One day you'll be as good as me!
To the most amazing Mum and Dad,
I'm sorry if I sent you mad.
To all the clients that made me smile,
I'll always go the extra mile.
A special thanks to Mr Jack,
You've made me laugh and had my back.
To the sleepless nights and crazy days,
I should have learned from my stubborn ways!
And to the Geordie girl who knows what I went through,
It will always be All About You!

First Printing, 2017

ISBN-13: 978-1541324473
ISBN-10: 1541324471

http://davidosgathorp.com

Cover design:
Interior design: Heather McIntyre, Cover&Layout www.coverandlayout.com

THE TRUSTED
TRAINER

CONTENTS

FOREWORD
A NOTE FROM THE AUTHOR

HELLO AND THANK you for buying my book, *The Trusted Trainer*. I sincerely hope that you enjoy reading it as much as I have enjoyed living it and documenting it. Wherever you currently are on your journey to establishing a successful health and fitness business, I'm confident that you can draw on my experiences, learn from my mistakes and take a shortcut to realising your own dream business!

This book is based around building great relationships and therefore I'm keen for your purchase of this book to mark the start of a great working relationship between us. I am always interested in speaking to new trainers and entrepreneurs about their businesses and, where necessary, provide a little business coaching or advice.

That's why I'd like to offer you a free 30 minute phone or Skype consultation to discuss anything that has struck a chord with you in The Trusted Trainer. I don't know how long I'll be able to offer this as the book sales take off but I will do my best!

And…

I'd also like to offer you free access to a network of personal training and health and fitness advice. You'll have the opportunity to pool information and resources with other trainers trying to make it in in the industry and develop your network of business contacts.

To take advantage of this, just send me an email: david@davidosgathorp.com with the subject 'Trusted Trainer' and I'll reply as soon as I can.

Thank you and good luck!

David
London, 2017

II THE TRUSTED TRAINER

INTRODUCTION

WELCOME TO THE Trusted Trainer, the step-by-step guide to attract, amaze and keep your personal training clients for life. The ideas in this book are all based on my own personal experiences. This is not something that has just been thrown together because it might give you a bit of success. These are all tried and tested solutions that will guarantee success when you follow them.

I'm not an overnight success; any success that I have had has been as a result of years and years of hard work, taking risks and making a hell of a lot of mistakes – and so, the good news is that you can learn from all of my struggles and take a shortcut to success. I enjoy getting all of my information from people who aren't guessing at how things should be done; I want it from a person who has gathered their information by searching the hard way, and that's exactly what I've done here.

My journey started in 2001 when I was fresh out of University and on the road to building my own business. Back then I didn't have a clear path to success, no mentor and no real idea of what I was doing! I believed that in order to be successful I had to get every qualification going, and so I studied relentlessly. I felt I had to gain experience in every possible field, so I worked in health clubs, private studios, hospitals, clinics, in schools and with sports teams, and I chose to work my ass off day after day, doing 18-hour day after 18-hour day, seven days per week for years…

It wasn't until a few years ago that I realised that whilst a strong work ethic and a determination to not give up is definitely important on the road to success, there is one thing that beats any of these traits hands down, and contributes far more to your chances of success in business and life, which is this:

That's it.

You can close this book now and just take that piece of advice with you, and I guarantee that if you live by that rule and you focus on building great relationships with people that come into your life then great opportunities will arise as a result.

If you want to keep reading then I'll do my best to keep you entertained. I'll divulge numerous tactics and strategies that are guaranteed to build stronger relationships with your clients, and from there my friend, the sky is the limit!

Before we really get stuck into things let me be clear on why this book talks about clients and not customers.

We'll dig into this in more detail in a later chapter, but for me, the definition of a customer is someone who buys goods or services from a business, whereas a client is someone who receives a professional service. Essentially, customers just buy the products you supply, while clients buy your advice and solutions that are personalised to their needs.

The way I see it, a customer is simply about the transaction. A client is someone who is under your care. If you just go after customers you can still have a good business, but if you aim to deliver a great service for your clients, gain their trust and build strong relationships with them, then you can have an amazing business!

Strong relationships are what all good organisations are built upon. In today's business world, the "Big R" is the key to everything. It's not what you know, it's who you know. A good education and a great smile will get you through the door for an interview, but if the guy sat next to you at that interview got there because his dad plays golf with the CEO, then your great smile isn't going to last long because there's only one winner in that game!

In sport, you need to have an incredibly high level of skill to "make it" to a professional level, but this alone doesn't guarantee success. There are a huge amount of incredibly skilful players out there who never had the opportunity to pursue a professional career within their chosen sport simply because they were never introduced to the right people at the right time who could make it happen.

The 80-20 rule states that 80% of your returns will come from 20% of your efforts, or put another way, 80% of your income will come from 20% of your clients. Often it's even more than this; take a close look at your numbers and if you follow the path of where each of your clients came from, they often lead back to the same one or two sources.

In the self-employed world one client can make or break your business. If you are lucky enough to meet that one client who wants to tell everyone about you (we often call these people connectors) then your business could explode as a result of the relationship you build with them. Later in this book we'll discuss how people like this can literally change your life, not just your business.

Look for these connectors. Go out of your way for them and always be looking for ways to build a relationship without any expectation. Change your mindset; don't look at what you can do in order to get something in return. The message of this book isn't give a little with the hope of something huge coming back to you. If you want to build a successful business then you should always look to give great service and experience with no expectation.

The key thing to remember is that you just don't know when opportunities may present themselves to you. I have recently had an introduction to a great business opportunity from someone that I have known for over five years. I've had no expectation for this whole time; I've just enjoyed building a great relationship with this person and now an amazing opportunity has arisen.

Every business succeeds or fails based on the number of people it is able to serve. The more people you serve, the more successful you will be – simple. With this in mind, most marketing strategies are based around getting more and more clients through the doors of your business. But is this all we have to do?

Just keep getting more and more people into your business?

Well in my opinion, NO. This actually isn't a great way of building a business. We focus so much on finding new clients, incentivising these new people and hitting those all-important sales targets week after week that we forget to actually deliver a proper service to these clients we work so hard to get through the door!

The result is they don't stay with you for particularly long and so your sales team (or more likely you) have to work even harder to get even more people through the door just to stand still! This is madness, and I've written this book to let you know that there is a much better way of doing things. A way that not only delivers the financial results that every business needs, but a service that clients will seek you out for and allow you to completely stand out from the crowd!

The truth is most businesses do a GOOD job of serving their clients, but in my opinion, a GOOD service isn't what any business should be striving to achieve. Often clients will keep going back to a "good" business simply because it's convenient, it's become a habit for them or because an alternative for them is simply too bad to be worth considering! If a GREAT business was to open up next door they would leave without a thought.

If your goal is to not be as bad as the terrible competition then I think you need to close the doors on your business now. You'll save yourself a lot of stress, time and money. If you want to build a successful business that you can be truly proud of then you have to really enjoy what you do, and you have to do something that no one else is doing. You have to seek out opportunities to wow your clients every single day.

If you can do this then I guarantee that your business will not only be more successful than you ever dreamed possible but you will love what you do, your business will energise you every day and you'll become a magnet for great clients, great trainers and great people in your life.

The message within this book is that if you want to build a business that grows year on year then you need to build great relationships that grow year on year!

It is my goal that a trainer new to the industry will pick up this book and my ideas will completely transform their outlook, and as a result their business and their life will go from strength to strength. I want you to realise that signing up for course after course to master your technical coaching skills will only take you so far: learning to really communicate with your clients is the real key to success.

As we'll discuss later in this book, there are so many great coaches out there who struggle to get any kind of career going, while there are many coaches with minimal qualifications who make a great living from this industry. These guys understand that real coaching is about delivering a service that enables the coach to build amazing relationships with their clients week after week and, as a result, building a business that can thrive for years.

Don't get me wrong; it is vital to gain as much knowledge as you can, but for me this only really matters when you combine that with the finer details and the professional experience that the client receives each time they step into the gym. It's about making the client feel like the most important person in your life for that hour that you spend with them. I named my business All About You to really emphasise this point. Most trainers get this so wrong; they want to be the star of the show, they only want to train their clients in the way that they train and they end up hurting their clients and their business.

I want this book to be a turning point for young coaches. To allow them to recognise that the level of success you have in this industry is directly correlated to the level of service that you are prepared to deliver.

Get your clients to know you, like you and ultimately trust you and your business and your life will go from strength to strength.

VIII   THE TRUSTED TRAINER

MY STORY

FOR MOST BUSINESS owners the decision to set up their own business often doesn't come purely from a positive desire to make a change, but from a negative experience that triggers something inside of them to do something different, to stop following someone else's rules and to become the master of their own destiny.

Often they can pinpoint a particular moment that changed everything for them and made them decide to take some massive action. Mine was when I started to work at a very exclusive health club in 2001. I was fresh out of University and I felt a real sense of achievement that I was using my Sport and Exercise Science degree and working for a company that had just been recognised as the best health club in London.

I soon found myself part of a great team of Sports Science graduates who all shared the same ideas and enthusiasm for the fitness industry; we were mentored under an incredible gym team manager and worked with the rich and famous of North London. I learnt a lot during these first few months and felt so proud to be part of this amazing organisation.

Then everything changed. A member of the team, a fantastic Kiwi girl, decided to move back home to New Zealand. A new guy was given the opportunity to replace her but immediately failed to impress me. During the following weeks I watched as he delivered really poor training sessions, looked completely uninterested while he was on the gym floor and basically everything about him was just mediocre!

I was angry and disappointed that this new team member had been allowed to join this excellent team and I felt he had let me and all of the other trainers down by delivering such a poor service. I told the management about this; they did nothing. I spoke to other members of the team about it; they all knew he was crap but didn't want to do anything about it, and so I decided that I had to change things.

I realised that I had a real problem with anyone who just couldn't be bothered to give 100%. I promised myself right then that I wouldn't accept mediocrity in my working life.

I left the health club and started up on my own and I loved not relying on anyone else; it was all down to me to deliver excellence and I thrived on that. I decided that opening my own business was the next logical step and the only way that I could guarantee the high standards that I felt clients deserved to receive.

All of my frustrations with my business since opening have been around others delivering mediocrity. I really believe that clients come into the studio with the opportunity to change their lives, and as health and fitness professionals we should not be prepared to let them down. My mission is to create the best health and fitness company in the country and I am not prepared to settle for anything else.

I have been to a huge amount of other gyms and studios all around the country and they are not as good as what my team and I have created. The level and ability of the training team we have now is vast, the facility is fantastic and we have the commitment from every member of the team to deliver excellence every day. Fortunately other people believe this as well and we were recently awarded Gym Team of The Year at The National Fitness Awards.

I want to create a centre of excellence. I want to create an experience that exceeds the expectations of our clients within a network of facilities that are at the forefront of the health and fitness world, delivering a service that is above all others in the industry.

My team and I can do this if we refuse to accept mediocrity; we only want to deliver excellence. We are not prepared to allow our clients to miss out on the opportunity to change their lives. We have the ability to create something truly amazing together and we are going to make that happen!

My philosophy is simply based on living with excellence and bringing a unique experience to each and every client session. I hope you can buy into this and make great things happen for yourself as a result. Enjoy the rest of the book…

CHAPTER 1
BEEN THERE, DONE IT, GOT THE T-SHIRT

THIS BOOK IS all about building relationships and so before we start I want you to get to know me, like what I've got to say and trust that it will yield results in your own business. Wherever you may be at this point in your business journey, you've picked this book up because you want to get a few ideas on building your personal training business, or you work at my studio and I've forced you to read it!

I was fortunate that I knew exactly what I wanted to do from a very young age. I was very passionate about sport; I dreamed of competing professionally but I fell short of that goal and managed to suffer a number of debilitating injuries that meant I had to find something else to do by my late teens. This was my first opportunity to recognise that everything happens for a reason, and as one door closes another one is always waiting for you to walk through.

I want this book to inspire someone out there to go after their goals and build the business of their dreams on the simple principle of having fun and building great relationships. Often the only thing that stands between you and your dream life is believing in yourself and taking that chance on you!

We tell ourselves that we can't do this; we can't achieve that, and the life that we dream of is way out of our reach, only reserved for the rich and famous.

I believe that's nonsense and that it doesn't matter where you've come from; it's all about where you want to go. The life that you want is yours if you dare to dream…

I moved to London in the summer of 2001 just two days after finishing university. I had my dream of building a successful business in the big city and I was so motivated, so positive, so eager to learn, so determined to make it happen, but sadly so skint I could barely afford to eat properly. I was living in a bed-sit in a really rough part of London and having to cash cheques in order to get me through until the end of the month.

The area I lived in was known for a big old football stadium, which was being rebuilt at the time. The rest of the surrounding area was incredibly run down and so rough that I used to get off the tube at 11pm after a very long day at work, strap on my back pack, get my head down and sprint the two miles home to avoid any conflict with the not-so-friendly locals who would be hanging round street corners at that time of night!

WHEN I WAS GROWING UP MY FAMILY WAS ~ SO POOR ~ { WE COULDN'T AFFORD TO PAY ATTENTION }

Looking back now, it was a pretty awful existence, but I never really thought of it that way. It was just something that I needed to do at that time in order to get me to where I wanted to be. Throughout this time I just kept my dream at the forefront of my mind and did all I could to move a step closer to it each day. I worked all hours, I got to know as many people as I could and I absorbed as much information as I could.

Today I tell all of the junior members of my team about the importance of continually learning. I watch them download courses, podcasts and audio books and it makes me smile. The youngsters these days don't know they're born!

I tell them my story, that before downloads there were these things called DVDs, and before DVDs there was something called video, and that's what my hard-earned money was spent on each week. If my dream was to be the best then I had to learn from the best and I realised early on that there was a lot I needed to learn.

I decided that I would have one client who would be my "Education Client" – the fact that he was a head teacher made this even more appropriate. Every penny that I earned from my education client went back into my own development. I went on courses, read every book I could get my hands on and yes, bought myself a lot of DVDs and video tapes!

These habits are ingrained in me now and I still continue to learn every week. These days it's more focused on building a business and I pay out thousands of pounds each year on courses, I read at least two books per week, I subscribe to a huge number of podcasts, newsletters, blogs and social media pages because my goal is to always aim to be the best at what I do.

I want to remain at the forefront of health and fitness, and I want to constantly know what's going on in my industry and to find inspiration from other companies, leaders and inspirational people in order to be able to offer my team and my clients more and more.

If you are reading this book then you have made, or soon will be making the transition from technician to business owner. This is an exciting journey and it will obviously mean that the emphasis shifts in the new things you're learning. Not only do you need to stay ahead of the game with your technical knowledge, but you also need to learn a whole new skill-set in running a business.

My advice throughout all of this is to enjoy the journey. It will inevitably take you a few years to establish a strong business, and you'll make a lot of mistakes along the way, but if you make a mistake once, don't worry about it. It's a chance to learn – just don't keep making the same mistakes!

Have fun along the way, build a business that you love going to, work with people that you love being around, stick to your guns, be clear about what you want to achieve and don't give up!

IF THE HAT FITS

If you want to attract and keep clients for life then you have to be the best version of yourself EVERY DAY!

By the way, when I refer to a business this may be a fifty person organisation or a one man band, it doesn't matter; the principles are the same.

There will be hundreds of new tasks that you'll have to do, most of which you have never received any training for and almost all of which you will hate doing! As a business owner you need to be the boss, the accountant, the head of marketing, the head of sales, the receptionist, the cleaner, the tea boy and a million other things whilst still being the best in town at what you do!

This means that you're going to need to start finding some good people to help you, because there's no way you can build a business that you love doing the things that you loathe.

So before we start anything you need to make a list of things that you LOVE doing and the things that you HATE doing. The things on the list you love are your new job description; the things on the list you loathe are going on your assistant's job description. If you think you can't afford an assistant then you need to remind yourself that this is your dream business and you need to just focus on doing what you love every day. You can find an assistant online who will cost you in a week what you can earn in an hour!

Make sure you take action and do this now!

It's your first step in not only building a business with actual staff, but also ensuring that you are able to consistently deliver exceptionally high standards to your clients. Attempting to do everything on your own will only lead to mistakes or getting burnt out, both of which have happened to me.

I know it's important to get my business to the top of Google but I don't want to learn how to do that.

I know it's important to create videos but I don't want to learn how to edit them.

I know it's important to have a great website and attention-grabbing flyers but I don't want to design them.

I know I need to keep my business spotlessly clean but I don't want to get the mop out!

I want to be a great coach.

I want to build a great business.

I want to offer all of my clients a great service.

And I want to enjoy my own free time doing what I really want to do.

This is just my outlook on things; it's not for everyone. Some people love the IT side of their business and some people take pride in doing everything within their business – if that is the case then who am I to stop you? If you're doing what you love then good on you!

The way I look at it my time is worth a lot to me. If I can charge £100 per hour for an hour's training session then why spend an hour doing something someone else can do better than me for a fraction of that price?

If I want any work done on my website or social media, any project research work done, any flyers designed, any videos edited and much more, I use my virtual assistant in India. You're a star by the way Ashvin!

The aim of this book is to show you how to build a great business based on delivering an exceptional, professional and personal service and how to attract, impress and keep clients coming back to you for life. It's definitely not about working your ass off doing shit you hate just to pay the bills!

If I've grabbed your attention then read on…I've got a lot more to share with you!

WHO AM I AND WHY SHOULD YOU LISTEN TO ME?

I've been in the industry for nearly 20 years, I've got all the boy scout badges, I've trained with some of the world-leading authorities on health and fitness and worked with some of the country's top physiotherapists, osteopaths and surgeons in my specialist field of corrective exercise, to create a thriving personal training business.

I work with numerous celebrity clients, I am the Human Performance Coach to the Red Bull Racing Formula One Team and I have my own personal training studios in London. I have a team of trainers and therapists working for me and we currently deliver over 1000 PT sessions each month. My company, All About You Personal Training, has recently won The Gym Team of the Year at the National Fitness Awards.

All of this has been achieved by first of all delivering an exceptional product that gets clients results, but also by going the extra mile and giving clients a truly unique experience that keeps them as "clients for life" and walking, talking adverts for me and my business.

More importantly than all of this is that I've made a huge number of mistakes along the way, and I've learned so many lessons from each of these that have made me a stronger businessman and, more importantly, a better person as a result.

I've employed the wrong people, worked with the wrong clients, allowed other people to make the wrong decisions in my business, taken terrible advice, taken on an investor who was very wrong for my business and it cost me a small fortune to buy them out. I've taken on a second studio that wasn't fit for purpose and had to move out when the floor fell through, and I lost £100,000 in the process. I've had people try to sue me, landlords try to screw me and taken risk after risk to build a business from nothing to multiple six figures in revenue.

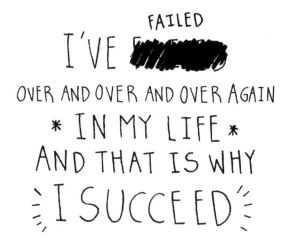

I've made ALL of the mistakes so you don't have to! I really do now know what I'm doing and I'm here to share all of this with you.

In order to be successful in the personal training industry you need to have a lot of clients – that's obvious. There are many ways of obtaining these clients; the old way of doing things via flyer drops, newspaper and magazine ads, billboards, talks, creating referral networks, building a great website then making it findable through Google AdWords campaigns, Facebook, YouTube, Twitter etc.

Each of these if done well should bring in clients and they are all marketing tools I have used myself to generate leads into my business.

I've spent a lot of time on all of this, and whilst I recognise that marketing my business is vitally important, my issue is that the more time I spend working on these things, the less time I get to do what I'm really passionate about and what I get a great buzz from. I got into this industry to do something I love, follow my dream, have fun, be a great coach and to build a great business, not to sit behind a keyboard.

Every trainer out there seems to be looking for the best way to attract more and more clients. All of the books and information products out there focus on how to attract more clients, creating shiny Facebook ads, sales page websites and flyers that will have clients banging down your door or creating a velvet rope approach to your business to position yourself as an expert and have clients really want to train with you. All of these things are important, but my message here is slightly different.

I have built my Personal Training business on a strong philosophy of "keeping clients for life".

This programme will outline that philosophy: it will tell you exactly what I do to wow my clients, how I make them feel special and more importantly, how you can learn to build strong relationships with your clients, make yourself part of their lives and literally get your clients to fall in love with your service so much they'll do the marketing for you!

I will discuss the importance of communication and going the extra mile, and give you a blueprint of exactly how to put these systems into practice now within your personal training business.

The general advice in the industry at the moment is if you want to earn more money from your fitness business you HAVE to run classes, boot camps and small group training.

I totally agree. If you want to leverage your time in the best possible way, have a positive effect on numerous people during one hour and you get a great buzz yourself from doing this then definitely go down that route. The ideas in this book can also help you build great relationships with your camp and class members.

My own personal outlook is that I don't really enjoy classes and small group training. It's just not my thing. I believe it definitely has its place, but I'm really passionate about working one-to-one with clients, really getting to understand how that individual's body works and what I can do to change what isn't working at the moment.

I'm a coach, I work one-to-one with my clients, and I keep them for a very long time because I get great results with them and build strong relationships with them. I also get numerous referrals from these clients and earn a very good living from my business.

The fact that I now have a team of coaches that follows the same principles I outline means that I can still have a huge impact on a large number of clients each week in a one-to-one setting.

I don't really see what my team of coaches do as being that out of the ordinary; it's just how I've always done things. It's only in the last few years that I've recognised the importance of documenting it and teaching it to my trainers because it doesn't come that naturally to everyone.

CHAPTER 2
THE FIRST DATE

YOU NEVER GET a second chance to make a first impression!
How different would your business be if you were to treat each meeting with a client like a first date?

I'm not encouraging anyone to literally start dating their clients, but imagine what would happen if you approached EVERY single training session with the same enthusiasm and attention to detail that you would on a first date with your dream partner?!

How much effort would you make to really try to impress them?

The biggest reason why most trainers lose clients is simply because they stop communicating effectively with their clients…Pretty much the same reason why ANY relationship breaks down!

Personal training: it's Personal with a capital "P" and training with a small "t".

Read that statement again! The actual training session you deliver to a client is just a small part of the service.

I always say to my team that Personal Training at All About You is Personal with a capital "P" and training with a small "t". In other words it should be a given that the training sessions are a very high standard, that they are specific to the client's needs, inventive, enjoyable, and most importantly deliver great results.

The big thing is the Personal element to the training session. If you've got the personality of a plank of wood – and believe me I've met a few trainers like that in my time – then unfortunately, you ain't gonna get too far in the fitness industry. If you can communicate effectively, understand your clients and provide the right solutions for them then you'll fly!

Over the course of your journey with your clients they will all inevitably go through a number of ups and downs that you will need to react to. Busy periods at work and the demands of their family life may take over from time to time, they may get injured or they may go through a time where they just lack motivation. All of these times are opportunities for a great trainer to be supportive, find a solution for the client or just be there to listen. Sadly this rarely happens; the trainer fails to deliver, the client loses interest and the relationship is lost. My goal is that by the time you finish this book you will NEVER let any of these things happen again!

Back to the first date; remember that excitement you had the first time you went out with that special someone? You made a big effort with the way you looked, the way you dressed and even the way you smelled? Get back to that place and re-live it in every session!

Why do trainers think that it's OK to fall out of bed, throw on some dirty clothes and walk around like a zombie sipping on their double espresso during a training session whilst trying to look interested?! You have the potential to charge similar fees to that of a decent accountant, so act with the professionalism that they have to.

CALL THEM JUST TO LISTEN

It's very sad but unfortunately most people just don't understand the concept of a conversation! The biggest mistake is that a hell of a lot of talking happens but very little listening goes on. Whilst one person is speaking the other is merely waiting for a break in the conversation to have their say.

When building a relationship, take note of the fact that you have two ears and one mouth!

Everyone wants to be heard but we rarely give people a chance to actually tell their story. If you want to build great relationships with your clients then just focus on this one piece of advice.

Listen to them.

Remember what they tell you.

Take a genuine interest in their life.

And aim to make a difference in whatever way that you can.

Make them feel as though they are the most important person in the room for the time that you spend with them. I wanted to really emphasise this point with my training team in my business and so I created a scenario to get them to really buy in…

My studio is located in a very affluent area of North London. We have a number of celebrity clients who train at the studio and an incredibly beautiful Hollywood actress recently moved to the area, and so the question was, "What would the quality of your session be like if Sienna Miller walked through the door and asked to train with you?"

From this question "Sienna Sessions" was created. The next question was, "How is Sienna Miller any different to any other client we see?" The answer is obviously that she shouldn't be; everyone who comes into the studio should be treated like a Hollywood superstar, be given the first date treatment at every session, build a relationship and become a client for life.

Go through our checklist below and see if you're regularly delivering Sienna Sessions to your clients.

"SIENNA SESSIONS"

At All About You it is our aim to deliver the perfect session with each client who comes in to the studio. Our personal training sessions involve a real PERSONAL experience. The target for all of the training team is to treat each client like a Hollywood A-lister and go the extra mile.

- The client will receive a text at least 24 hours before the session confirming the appointment and letting them know that you are looking forward to seeing them.
- You will arrive at the studio at least 10 minutes before the session.
- You will be dressed well in full All About You uniform, well groomed, looking good, feeling good and smelling good!
- You will leave all of your personal issues at the door and ensure you are always in a positive frame of mind when working at the studio.
- Your training sessions will always be well thought out, progressive and personal to your client's unique goals.
- Trainers will always get their client's water for them; they will offer them a towel and go out of their way to serve them.
- Your training sessions will be positive and although you will aim to push your clients to their physical limits you will always deliver an enjoyable experience.
- Your aim in each session is to build on the relationship with your client.
- Take the time to listen to your clients and understand exactly what they want.
- Every training session is a "Date", so make them fall in love with you (not literally)!!
- At the end of the session thank them for coming in.
- Take action on any requests they have made during the session or refer their requests to the relevant person to deal with.
- Confirm the time and day of your next appointment at the end of your session.

- See them to the door and wish them a good day.
- Make a note of anything that came up in the session that you can act on in order to go the extra mile.
- Email them later that day ensuring they had a good session and attach any "homework" reports or ideas you have for them.

CHAPTER 3
WOW THEM

THE KEY TO any relationship is for your client to get to know you, like you and obviously trust you. Trust can take a while, but they can form an instant impression of whether they want to get to know and like you.

Trainers often believe that it's all about the programme they deliver. In my opinion that's the last thing that you need to worry about. The truth is, even a half-decent programme will get results if someone is continually pushing themselves beyond their previous best and following it consistently. The key to success for personal trainers is to build a really strong relationship with each client and show them that you really want to help them achieve their goals because:

?

NO ONE CARES
~ HOW MUCH YOU KNOW ~
UNTIL THEY KNOW
HOW MUCH YOU CARE!

Once a client knows how much you care about them then the real progress can begin. With each session your aim is to try to impress your client more and more. You are showing them that what they have bought is more than an hour of your time; it's a promise to give them top level coaching, guidance and support in order to help them achieve their specific goal and a commitment to go the extra mile at every opportunity. Do this and you gain their trust completely, and the relationship can really start to progress from here.

Have you ever been to a coffee shop and the barista remembered your order from last time and made you the drink before you even asked? That's a WOW in my book. There are four coffee shops on my high street and to be honest the one I go to probably doesn't serve the best coffee, but the service is head and shoulders above the others; that's the only reason I go back!

On the flip side, have you ever been to a restaurant where the food was incredible and the wine was out of this world but the waitress was just rude and turned the whole evening sour?

I'm sure we've all had these experiences and this is why I honestly believe that the product you deliver as a personal trainer – i.e. the training programme – is just a small part of the whole package.

The restaurant with the best chef in town can end up being the place to avoid if the staff who are serving his food are not up to standard, and likewise an average product, like the cup of coffee, can become amazing when it's delivered with five star service.

Let me share this one simple trick to wow your clients at every session: Take five minutes after each session to make some notes.

That's it!

OK let me share a bit more with you…During those five minutes you need to note down every important conversation that came up in that session.

THE CHECK LIST:
- How was your client today?
- What is going on in their life at the moment?
- Are their kids doing well?
- What are the names of their kids?
- What is going on in their work life?
- Where do they work?
- Are they working on an important project?
- Are they looking for a new job?
- Are they studying towards a new career?
- What are they doing at the weekend?
- Where are they going on holiday?
- What have they told you they are interested in?

I can go on but I think you get the idea. Those few minutes just after your session are a great opportunity to really wow your client at the next meeting.

The reason why this works is because sadly most people are terrible at this! Husbands forget wives' birthdays, friends forget about nights out they had planned, work colleagues forget to complete those important tasks. Day after day people experience disappointment on some level and so the act of remembering the smallest thing goes a huge way to building great relationships.

Showing someone that you actually listened to them and remembered something they said they were doing will enable you to stand out from most people in their circle. Try it now: take out a pen and paper or open up notes on your mobile phone and write down five things you know about one or two of your clients. If you struggle with this exercise then you've got some work to do.

EXERCISE
THE END OF SESSION REVIEW:

How was your client feeling today?

What is going on in their life at the moment?

What are they struggling most with at the moment?

How can you help them the most at this time?

What excitement have they got planned?

What are they doing before they see you next?

What new thing have you learned about them today?

What part of the training session did they respond to really well today?

What suggestions did you make for goals for the next session?

What can you do right now to maintain their motivation for training with you?

CHAPTER 4
THE F**KING WOW!

WE'RE STEPPING THINGS up again. Every session is still a first date, every interaction is an opportunity to wow your clients, the end of every session is a time to reflect and note down those little nuggets of information that will make your relationships with your clients even stronger, but you can do even better than that, can't you?

Once you've been working with clients for a few months, they've had the chance to get to KNOW you, they hopefully LIKE you and you're beginning to build up TRUST with them; now it's time to really WOW them..!

Take out your notes, read through them and take the time to work out what you can do for this client to really blow them away.

I want you to buy them a gift to celebrate the results that they have achieved with you so far, and to show them that you really value them as a client and that you genuinely care that they do well.

The value of this gift is up to you but before you decide let me share some basic maths with you.

The average personal training session will cost somewhere around £50 per hour.

Your client will see you on average once per week.

They will go on holiday for a few weeks per year, you will go on holiday a few weeks per year (hopefully!) –they will cancel sometimes and you may have other commitments, but for argument's sake, let's say you see them forty times per year.

£50 x 40 weeks = £2000 per year.

If you're doing your job right and following all of the advice in this book then they should stay with you for at least two years. So that client is worth £4000 to you.

If you just spent 1% of that amount on them you could really f**king wow them!

A 1% investment of what you can easily earn from them will be the best money you've ever spent.

Ideas for your f**king wow present:

You want the present to be something that they will see often and think of you, or for it to be an experience that they possibly share with you that they can remember for a long time…

I have given clients workout clothes, trainers, heart rate monitors, sports watches and exercise equipment so that every time they exercise they think about me. These presents have always been well received, but I now try to give gifts that are not related to fitness.

My goal is to be a big part of my client's life and I also see my role as a coach, not just a fitness trainer, but that conversation is for another time.

I now give clients gifts that they can enjoy away from the gym. I give them theatre tickets, tickets to sporting events, I book pamper days for them at a spa or I take them out for dinner.

If you think this is over the top then let me tell you about a little thing called marketing that every business needs to rely on if it is going to succeed.

Most people would say that if you want to get more leads for your business then the easiest way of doing this is to put out flyers to advertise your business. So they take the time to create the copy to go on the flyer, they then send it to a designer and pay for them to make it look pretty, the designer then sends it over to the printer who will churn out thousands of copies of your pretty new flyer and then you'll pay someone to deliver these flyers for you – or worse than that, you'll spend hours actually delivering them yourself!

Let's do the maths on this "obvious" marketing exercise:

Time to write the copy for the flyer – 2 hours minimum (don't you charge £50 per hour?)

Flyer to be professionally designed – £100

Flyers to be printed – £200

Flyers to be delivered – £100

These are fairly conservative estimates on costs but as you can see, we're easily up to £400 with a lot of your time invested in this process.

Now, here's the best thing: do you know what the predicted lead generation is from flyer delivery?

1% is generally a pretty good return!

A 1% return to generate people you know nothing about doesn't seem like a great deal to me.

Remember the other 1% number we discussed earlier though? Investing just 1% of the income you can easily expect to generate from your favourite clients will not only build the relationship with them but do you think they'll tell a few people about the experience? Do you think people will notice the great results they are achieving and ask them what they are doing? Do you think that those clients you love training will hang out with similar people you'd love to train? And do you think that if you just ask these clients to refer some of their friends to you they will do whatever they can to help you grow your business?

F**king wow your clients at every opportunity and you will build amazing relationships and build your business at the same time, with clients who will be drawn to you because of the great things they are constantly hearing about you from their friends.

It's such a simple thing to do but most trainers will NEVER consider this option because they only think of short-term, quick-fix solutions. As a result they create CUSTOMERS who pay them for a simple transaction, not CLIENTS who invest in a long term relationship. Play the long game. EXPECT to have every client for at least two years and look after that investment at every opportunity.

Let me share a story with you...

The wife of a client of mine has recently set up new business designing jewellery. He was telling me that she met with a graphic designer to help her to design a logo for the business. Over the phone this girl quoted £600 for the work and promised that it would be delivered within a week.

The girl then came round to the house to spend some time with my client's wife to discuss the business and getting a better picture of what kind of design would work for her.

Two weeks later (not one week as promised) a completely different design was sent, along with a bill for £1400!

My client and his wife live in a very large family home in North London. They have a brand new Range Rover Sport sat on the driveway and some beautiful art and collectors' items within their home.

Obviously the graphic designer saw all of this and, with a very narrow-minded approach, simply decided to more than double her quote. Why do people do this? It may be a quick win but by not sticking to your word you destroy a relationship before it has a chance to develop.

My client's wife is a real social butterfly in North London. If she likes what you do then everyone knows about it! She could have sent thousands of pounds of additional work to the graphic designer; instead she'll never refer her to anyone and won't use her service again either.

A f**king wow is very often just doing what you say you will do!

Your aim should be to under-promise, over-deliver and look for the long-term relationship – it will always be worth more!

CHAPTER 5
HAVE THE SOLUTION

ALWAYS REMEMBER THAT your client first made contact with you because they had a problem and they believed that YOU had the solution. After working with them for a number of months you've hopefully provided the solution for them, and as a result you've built up a great level of trust with them. So what can you do to build upon this?

Keep solving problems for them!

Solve problems with their training and nutrition goals, solve problems with their sleep issues, their aches and pains, their recovery strategies and even with what they wear to the gym, and then look at ways to solve other problems in their life.

Do you have a list of local contacts? If your client needs to see a physiotherapist or osteopath do you have the details of someone for them? If they need a treatment for any reason be part of that process by recommending someone local and offering to contact the practitioner to speak to them about your client's issues. As well as adding value to your service you may find it also ends up being a useful referral source to bring new clients to your business.

I began doing this many years before I even opened my business and now I've built great relationships with some amazing therapists and medical specialists in London as a result. Now, not only am I able to liaise effectively with them for the benefit of my clients, but they believe in my business and really trust my team of coaches. As a result they have become a fantastic source of referrals for new clients for my business!

Do you know everyone in your area?

It's not only therapists that you should know; be the solution to all of your client's needs. Do you know an electrician, a plumber, a beautician, even a window cleaner?

Having a list of contacts like this will make you SO valuable to your clients.

And it benefits you in two really good ways…

Firstly, you become the go to person when they have a problem, and when you solve that problem their opinion of you just gets better and better.

Secondly, each person on your list becomes a new source of potential clients for you, if you take the time to personally meet with each of these people, get them in to do jobs at your home or your business, tell them all about what you do and what you're hoping to achieve and maybe incentivise them to send clients your way.

Don't just limit this idea to health and fitness professionals. People are always looking for problems to be solved at home. They need builders, plumbers and electricians they can trust. Build your list of contacts and solve problems; this is an amazing opportunity for you to find solutions and solve problems. Trust me, this really works.

When someone you trust tells you about a business or service that you should try then you are significantly more likely to contact them rather than an unknown business found on Google.

SO, make sure that your contact list is full of GREAT individuals and businesses, and more importantly ensure that your own service is the best that it can be. Working like this ensures a win, win, win arrangement. Your client wins, your "business partner" wins and you win by simply making an introduction!

Just having their contact details will make you useful to your clients; going to visit all of these businesses and building relationships with them makes them really useful to you.

CONTACT NUMBERS

NAME/BUSINESS	NUMBER	ADDITIONAL INFO
CARPENTER		
ELECTRICIAN		
PLUMBER		
HANDYMAN		
BEAUTICIAN		
PHYSIOTHERAPIST		
OSTEOPATH		
HAIRDRESSER		
DRY CLEANER		
PRINTERS		
MASSAGE THERAPIST		
ALTERNATIVE THERAPIST		
DENTIST		
LOCKSMITH		
MOT CENTRE		
GP SURGERY		
SPECIALIST FOOTWEAR		
LOCAL SPORTS SHOP		
HOME FITNESS EQUIPMENT		
SUPPLEMENTS COMPANY		
HEALTH FOOD SHOP		

CHAPTER 6
WHAT TYPE OF TRAINER ARE YOU?

LET'S TAKE A break from focusing on the client and take a quick look at you as a trainer. I want you to work out exactly what type of trainer you are and what you want to achieve from the fitness industry. This is a time to get really honest with yourself and decide whether you really want to build a career in this field or if this is something that you want to do for a little while before you pursue a "proper career".

I started working in gyms while I was at college and university and for me it never felt like work. While I saw friends of mine dragging themselves off to stack shelves in a supermarket or work behind a bar until the early hours I always loved heading in for my shifts at the gym. I loved the buzz of a busy gym floor, I loved being around people that wanted to exercise and push themselves and I built great friendships with the like-minded people who I worked with; what was there not to like?!

Moving to London and starting my own business was all I wanted to do from a young age but I have had to be so strong and determined to keep going with it over the years. There have been so many occasions over the last few years when most people would have given up because things just got too tough, but I couldn't because I have always been so committed to this life.

I've really struggled with girlfriends not understanding why I wanted to work so hard instead of staying in and watching *Made in Chelsea* with them!

I've had friends questioning my work hours and even mocking me for following my passion rather than giving up on a dream and just following them into the rat race.

I've even had some of my clients asking when I was going to get a proper job?! They meant it as a compliment because they thought I was an intelligent guy who could do more than be "just a trainer" but I always believed that I could achieve everything I wanted by working for myself in an industry I love.

Inevitably, after working so hard for years and things maybe not coming together as I would have hoped, you start to question yourself and think that maybe the doubters are actually right…The early starts, the late nights, the weekends and the fact that you never really switch off from things, why would anyone really want to do this?

YOU HAVE TO BE ODD TO BE NUMBER ONE

Well, I still do.

My business still gives me a lot more than it takes away but I understand why people want to get out. Why they want something more stable, a 9-5, a steady wage, no early starts, no late nights, no weekends and the ability to switch off when they walk out at the end of the day instead of managing the constant stress of running their own business.

This industry is tough. You WILL question why you work so hard, why you get up so early, why you work so late and why you give so much. There will be times when you don't earn enough and when you have to put up with clients that you don't even like.

And so the question is, do you REALLY want to work in this industry or is it just something that you think you want to do right now? If you're serious about it then keep going, believe in yourself, work harder than is required, risk more than you feel comfortable with, dream big, be strong and never give up, and you will thrive in what I honestly believe is the best career in the world!

Through the tough times there was one quote that got me through. I even got this printed on the wall in my office at the gym:

"When you feel like quitting, remember why you started."

If this chapter has struck a chord, if you're having a tough time and you're unsure whether this is what you really want, then just do yourself a favour and get out now. You can achieve anything you want from this industry if you're prepared to give everything, but if you can't, then take this piece of advice from my book: walk away now and don't look back!

If you're still with me then let me share a story with you of the types of people that I'm sure you've come across in various gyms across the world. It doesn't matter where you may be; these people will always show up! From my experience, I've worked in numerous health clubs, gyms, injury clinics and personal training studios, and basically worked out that there are FIVE main types of personal trainers out there.

Before you open your own business decide if you really are "number five" and use this again when you start to recruit your own team of trainers.

THE DRIFTER

The trainer who doesn't really know what they want to do with their life; they enjoy health and fitness and think that it could be an easy job for them. They like keeping fit, they know a few people who have done well in this industry and so they're going to give it a go because they don't really know what else they want to do.

THE TRAINING FREAK

We all enjoy our training but this guy is purely in the industry for his gain. He works in the gym because it means he can train whenever he wants and almost resents it when clients turn up on his time. He's also usually had a personality by-pass and isn't the most intelligent fella you've ever met.

THE STEADY EDDY

This guy is a good trainer. His clients like him and he makes a decent living from the industry but he's not willing to put in the hard work to really build a great business. He'll probably drop out and get a 9-5 job that's safer.

THE DREAMER

This guy is a great trainer, he's really passionate about what he does, his clients love him and he earns a fairly good living from the industry. He has loads of great ideas for what he can do with his business and talks a lot about them but never gets round to actually doing them and becomes frustrated. As a very successful client of mine used to say, this guy needs to "shit or get off the pot".

THE PT BUSINESS MAN

This guy may have been in the position of any of the other guys at some point but there has been a light bulb moment and he has realised that he can achieve great things in the industry by having the balls to go out there and do it. He has a clear vision of what he wants, a clear plan of how to do it and the drive and passion to do it!

If you haven't got the mindset to be the PT Business Man then this book is probably not going to make much difference. If you can do the one thing that most trainers fail to do – which is to run your business like a business – then you'll do very well. Stand out from the crowd and go the extra mile in your business and you'll be very successful. Stick with it, believe in yourself and always remember why you started.

FAILING TO PLAN IS PLANNING TO FAIL

The different trainers outlined above struggle to make it in this industry because they don't really understand the key to building a successful business. Most Personal Trainers have very little business acumen and there is seldom an actual plan of what they want the business to achieve, what they personally want to achieve and how they will measure this success.

Just remember, you need to put the hard work in if you want to be successful in this industry, or any other for that matter. I find it very hard to deal with trainers in this industry who are constantly looking for the easy wins by conning their clients – these types of people go against everything I stand for.

If you are going to create an amazing service for your business then don't do the following things:

Don't tell your clients they have to train a minimum of four times per week because you're not able to go out and fill your diary by any other means.

Don't sell your clients unnecessary supplements in order to make a bit of extra cash on the side.

Don't make your client do your workout with you because you didn't get the chance to train properly today!

Don't sit on the floor drinking coffee, looking bored and just counting reps! Yes, I've actually seen this happen.

Don't copy a workout you found online that morning because you were too lazy to actually prepare a proper training programme for them.

Don't come back from a one day course and believe you're an expert in anything, but don't stop going on one day workshops because you don't believe you can learn anything from them either!

Always be professional, always put the client's needs first and always be looking for ways to better yourself. The path of excellence is always a continuous journey.

If you are looking for the quick fix then again, please stop reading here. It's taken me ten years to be an overnight success. I want it to take you a lot less time than it's taken me, but it's not going to happen instantly and if it does you won't appreciate it enough or be prepared to deal with it.

THE PATH OF EXCELLENCE

Excellence is the quality of consistently surpassing ordinary standards. In order to be truly excellent at anything you need to have an incredibly clear definition of what excellence is to you, what it will look like in your life and how you will measure it.

As I stated at the start of this book, if your goal is to not be as bad as the competition then what is the point? An average business can only give you an average life. A consistently excellent business will guarantee you an excellent life, so ask yourself what do you really want?

Excellence requires a different kind of mindset; it needs a commitment to consistently go beyond your previous best. It requires you to focus on it intensely, day in and day out, always keeping a clear picture of exactly what you must do to achieve the level of excellence you honestly want in your life.

Determine what excellence looks like to you. Be clear what an excellent business, an excellent income, an excellent lifestyle and excellent relationships look like to you and then create a plan to move your life in that direction.

This is the difficult bit; you need to exhibit a level of discipline that most people are unwilling to commit to. Many people will talk about excellence; many will say they want to be more successful, happier, more fulfilled but is only those who are prepared to apply consistent discipline that are able to turn their plan into reality.

Be focused, be committed, be clear about everything that you want and be consistently excellent!

CHAPTER 7
WHAT DOES YOUR BUSINESS LOOK LIKE?

START WITH WHY

IF YOU ONLY read one book this year (other than this amazing little book, obviously!) then make it *Start with Why* by Simon Sinek. This book was a bit of a game-changer for me. Not only did it give me more focus for how I wanted my business to be run but it also made me realise the type of leader that I wanted to become.

The book is based on the concept that most businesses know WHAT they do and HOW they do it but very few know WHY they do what they do. Isn't this true to life in so many ways?

Knowing your WHY is the key to success for yourself as the business owner, for the people that you employ and most importantly for the clients that buy into that WHY!

Going back to the previous discussing "What type of trainer are you?" it's easy to see that only one type of trainer on that list would know WHY they do what they do, WHY they want to build their business in a certain way and WHY all of that is so important to them.

When you know why you are getting out of bed in the morning then every decision you make becomes easy.

You need to have a purpose; you need to believe in what you're doing and really believe in yourself, but more importantly, believe in something bigger than yourself.

As you grow your business, not only do you have to know WHY you are doing this, but you also need to be able to sell this dream to those who come and work with you. You don't need to force your views down other people's throats and turn them into mini clones of yourself, BUT you do need to sell them on the reasons why working within your business is going to be more beneficial to them than working on their own.

As I said at the start of this book I've made a huge number of mistakes over the last ten years, but the one that stands out above all others – and the main reason why numerous other mistakes were made – is the fact that I didn't have a clear vision for my business from day one.

I was a cocky young guy who was a great trainer and who attracted good people towards him. I was bored of working in the big box gyms and I grew tired of running someone else's business. I had a great following and I just thought, why don't I set up my own business? It can't be that difficult can it?

Well at the start it wasn't that difficult. I had my own shiny new converted warehouse space. I was fully booked within a few months and so I brought a really good friend on board to help me out. Looking back, that was a great time; I had no expectations for the business, I was working with some great clients and had a mate there to support me, and we had a lot of fun.

Then he got really busy and so we took on another trainer, and he got busy and we took on another trainer! Almost overnight we went from a couple of friends having fun working together to a proper business, and it was only at this stage after a few years that I started to think that I could create something really special.

Fast forward a few years, and a few bad recruitment decisions, a few very difficult clients, a shocking decision to bring an investor into the business, a failed second studio, a law suit, three extensions on my premises and a lot of money wasted and I'm now clear on what I want from my business!

Like I said, I've made every mistake in the book but I've learned a valuable lesson each time and now I am clear on exactly the type of business that I want, the culture that I want to create within the business, the type of clients that I want to serve and how and where I will expand the business in the future.

I'm going to share some of these ideas with you here.

My vision will probably not align with your vision; how can it? I'm sure we are very different people, I'm sure we look very different, I'm sure we think about things in a very different way and as a result we see the world very differently, and so what is right for me may be very wrong for you, but feel free to use the structure of my business to support your ideas.

MY TEAM CULTURE

If you are going to set up your own business then you are going to be spending a lot of time in one place, so you HAVE to make sure that you create a positive culture amongst your team of trainers and clients. A business only gets stressful and hard when you are doing things you don't like doing or surrounding yourself with people that you don't like being with!

You need to determine what values are most important to you and stick to them. Your working life will only really get tough when you are going against what you truly believe in. If you are going into a business that works in a manner that reflects your personality, and you've brought people into the business who support you and work towards your shared goal, then every day is easy, everything flows smoothly and success is easily achievable.

I created the diagram above to reflect the eight key areas that I think are most important in building a great team. I believe that if you have all of these things working simultaneously then success is pretty much guaranteed!

Let me explain a bit more and put into context how these traits can drastically improve your ability to attract and keep your clients for life...

My Team Culture at All About You is based on eight key areas:

1. Integrity – Always do what you say you're going to do.
2. Better people make better Team members. Always aim to be better today than you were yesterday.
3. Education – If you're not growing anywhere, you're not going anywhere.
4. Be Prepared to Fail – The only way to succeed is to fail! If you're not failing enough then you're not challenging yourself enough.
5. Give back – Show a sense of appreciation.
6. Team Time – We are a TEAM, not a group of individuals.
7. The Extra Mile – Winners always do extra.
8. Communication – Understand and be understood, and always be interesting and interested.

INTEGRITY

The best definition of integrity I ever heard was "always doing the right thing, even when no one is watching."

Unfortunately people let you down; they say they will do something and they forget. They promise they will be there for you and they don't turn up. They say they will come round to help you out and then it slips their mind. Most of the time there are genuine and good reasons for people letting you down.

If I can give you one tip for really standing out from the crowd then just DO WHAT YOU SAY YOU ARE GOING TO DO! We have all been guilty of saying we'll do something for someone and then simply forgetting. Live with integrity; actually do what you say you are going to do. Keep a promise and you will go very far in life!

BETTER PEOPLE

Always strive to better yourself. Your life should be a continuous path of excellence and your aim should always be to be a better person today than you were yesterday. Strive to improve yourself in all areas of your life and place other people's needs ahead of your own.

BE PREPARED TO FAIL

When you take risks you learn that sometimes there will be times when you succeed and times when you fail, but both are equally important. Don't stand still – just take a small step outside of your comfort zone and wait for the magic to happen!

GIVE BACK

We make a living by what we get but we make a life by what we give. Doing more for others than you do for yourself is a real success.

TEAM TIME

Always find time to spend with your team mates. Even if you are a one man band you can still build a powerful team. Build relationships with businesses, other trainers, other therapists and local businesses. Don't try to do it all on your own. Alone you can do so little; together you can do so much.

THE EXTRA MILE

The extra mile is a magical place that so many people have never discovered. We get used to receiving and delivering the bare minimum in all aspects of our life. Poor service, terrible communication and constant negativity are daily experiences. Make someone smile, do something nice just for the hell of it, wow them and I guarantee it will make you feel as good as them!

COMMUNICATION

Be clear, concise and always present, remember that you have two ears and one mouth so learn how to listen more and talk less, and always aim to be interesting and interested. Effective communication is essential in every element of life.

CHAPTER 8
JOHN SMITH

YOU'RE PROBABLY REALISING by now that I'm one of those annoying guys who loves a motivational quote! I'm not the type that feels the need to take to social media and tell the world how amazing life is just because I went for a 20-minute jog this morning, but I do think that some quotes just really hit the spot and sum up in a few simple words a different way to look at life. One of my favourite quotes is this one:

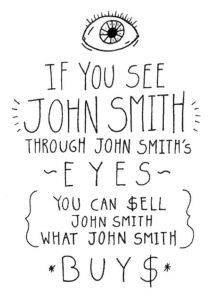

IF YOU SEE
JOHN SMITH
THROUGH JOHN SMITH's
~EYES~
{ YOU CAN $ELL
JOHN SMITH
WHAT JOHN SMITH }
BUY$

Remember this little phrase when you see each of your clients and I guarantee your relationship with them will improve. In my years of training, the one thing that really strikes me most is the fact that so many people have no concept of empathy.

The client hasn't come to you because they look at the world in exactly the same way as you. They've come to you because they don't know what to do, because they want to learn, because they've had a bad experience in the past and because they trust that you can really help them. So please try to see the world through their eyes, work out exactly what they want to get from training with you and then deliver it.

In my opinion the simple approach of one size fits all has to be dismissed. One size fits no one when it comes to delivering a personal service and building strong relationships. I'm sure that there are a lot of group fitness instructors out there who completely disagree with my opinion, but I just don't see how any two people can have exactly the same needs, so how can they get the most out of their investment in you?

The needs of a 21-year-old type A man are going to be very different to those of a 55-year-old woman who hasn't exercised for years.

Yes, they both need to move more.

Yes, they both need to move more effectively.

Yes, they both need to eat better.

And yes, they will both need to make changes to their current lifestyles.

BUT, how they move, how they eat and how they live their lives are going to be SO different. Giving them both the same solution is just madness in my eyes, but I see it all the time.

Step back for a minute, put yourself in your client's shoes and deliver them exactly what they want and need.

Get the big picture perspective on each of your clients and ask yourself these two questions:

What do they REALLY want from seeing you?

Is it to feel more attractive, to release a lot of anger they have inside of them, to live longer, or just to have someone to talk to? These aren't answers that are going to come up in your first consultation; this will take time to come to the surface. Once it does then you can really help your client achieve this goal. So the second question you need to ask yourself is:

What can I do to build trust with my client today?

Before you throw together a programme that will kick their ass and leave them unable to walk upstairs for a week, stop and see the world through their eyes, see what your client really wants, understand why they have really come to see you and then sell it to them.

CHAPTER 9
THE FEMININE TOUCH

SO YOU'VE GOT yourself a busy diary, you've opened up your own studio, you're really successful and everyone is going to be banging down your door to work with you. Follow the advice in this book and I guarantee they will! Just make sure you get it right when they turn up…

The most common way that trainers lose clients is often by just doing the simple things wrong.

The gym floor is where great things happen. Fat is burned and pride is earned! Bodies are sculpted, personal bests are reached and dreams are realised. It's a fantastic environment to be around; there is a real buzz and an enjoyment factor that is really addictive.

There's also the other side; the blood, sweat and tears…

Injuries can and probably will happen at some stage on the gym floor; it can also become a place where people release a lot of pent up anger and frustration and it's definitely going to get smelly and sweaty.

Remember that 21-year-old guy that you love training because he beasts himself every time he comes in? He could be repelling your 55-year-old female client who hasn't exercised for years because he's left a trail of sweat all around the gym and he stinks! His choice in music may massively offend her and his dirty trainers have left mud all over the floor where she usually stretches.

If this is the case then it doesn't matter how good your training session is going to be, how much you've really thought about what your client wants and how attentive you are in the session – you've lost them.

So what do you do in this situation?

There are two simple solutions here, simple but not easy…

If the guy described above is something that you've come across in the past then you need to determine whether he is your ideal client or if the 55-year-old lady is who you want to aim your services at. If the 21-year-old guy is representative of all of the other clients you have at your studio then I'm sure a packet of anti-bacterial wipes and a can of Febreze will do the job and everyone can just get on with it!

If your 55-year-old female client is representative of your typical client then you need to keep her and clients like her happy as your priority!

It may be time to choose to train one type of client or the other, but that's a whole other subject that we'll address later.

The second simple solution is to plan your diary effectively.

Give yourself fifteen minutes between sessions and this will give you the time to eat, drink, go to the toilet, reply to any urgent messages and go through your post-session check list!

- Wipe down all equipment used
- Spray air freshener
- Choose appropriate music for your next client
- Sweep or wipe the floor
- Get ready for show time!

Again, this may be obvious information but as we'll discuss later on, the small things will always be the big things. Forget about what you think is "good enough" for a training environment; when it comes to keeping clients happy in any business it all comes down to two things:

CLEANLINESS AND FRIENDLINESS

Here's the way we do things at All About You to make sure those things happen each and every time.

ALL ABOUT YOU
HIGHGATE

YOUR PRE SESSION
CHECKLIST

▶ Ensure your training session is properly booked in on EZ Facility.

▶ Confirm the training session with your client at least 24 hours before hand.

▶ Always arrive at least 10 minutes before your session begins.

▶ Act as if no one else will be at the studio, no matter what time of day it is.

▶ Prepare the studio, lights on, machines on, TV's and music on (appropriate for all clients) everything is how it should be.

▶ Deal with any problems before your client arrives.

▶ Prepare yourself for show time!

ALL ABOUT YOU
HIGHGATE

YOUR POST SESSION
CHECKLIST

III▶   Confirm the time and day for your next session.

III▶   See your client to the door and thank them for training
          with you.

III▶   Put all equipment you have used during the session
          back where you found it.

III▶   Wipe down all mats and machines used by your client.

III▶   Throw away their cups and towel roll and put any
          used towels in the washing basket.

III▶   Give yourself a moment to breathe, eat, renew and
          get back out there!

III▶   Check off your session as attended on EZ Facility.

CHAPTER 10
THE RESTAURANT TOILET

DON'T BELIEVE ME about the last chapter? Picture the scene; you've been told about this great new restaurant in town.

The food is amazing.

The staff are really attentive and friendly.

The cocktails are incredible.

The place looks amazing, and your friends have told you numerous times that you just have to go and try it out.

So you book a table and the food IS amazing. The staff really ARE friendly and attentive. The cocktails are the best you've EVER had and the place DOES look amazing, and so you decide that you're going to tell ALL of your friends about this place!

Until you go to the toilet at the end of the night…

The smell makes you feel sick.

The floor is soaking wet, the lock doesn't work properly, there's no toilet roll, the bin is overflowing, there are no hand towels and you don't even want to touch the door handle as you get out of there as quickly as possible with the thought that just won't go away…

If that's what their toilet looks like, then what on earth does their kitchen look like?!

So right then you decide that you're never going back there again.

A service industry is made or destroyed on the smaller things. Get them right and you'll have clients for life and with it, massive success with your business. Mess them up and your dream business will quickly turn into a nightmare.

Fact.

CHAPTER 11
GIVE AWAY SOMETHING BIG

IT'S ALWAYS BEEN a goal of mine to make my business a focal point of the local community. I get involved in local matters, I know the big events that are affecting the local people, I attend meetings to find out more and to show my support and I buy locally (even though it usually costs me more).

It was always my goal to build relationships with local businesses, to work with the local schools and to be involved in local charitable causes.

My business is very supportive of other local businesses and has become a big part of the local community; we have also formed great relationships with the local schools and are currently delivering eight PE classes per week both at my studios and within the school facilities.

Our charity projects grow year on year and in the last few years we have set up fun runs, fitness challenges and 24-hour endurance events. We've raised a lot of money for some great causes and in return received a lot of publicity. For one event we even managed to get on the ITV 6 o'clock news. Some great achievements there, but it's been a hell of a lot of work.

There are easy wins out there as well. Donating a prize to a local charity is always a great way to "do your bit" but make sure you do it in the right way.

When I first opened my studio I had a client who was organising a school fayre for her child's school and she was responsible for getting raffle prizes for the event. She approached me and I kindly donated one Personal Training session with me.

I walked away feeling great about myself, thinking that everyone would love that, they would be desperate to get in to book their session with me and then obviously beg to sign up for three sessions per week as soon as they'd met me. What an amazing, charitable guy I was and what a fantastic marketing idea this could be. I was so happy with myself I approached a few other schools to make them the same offer.

But something strange happened…

No one ever turned up! It took me a long time to work out why this genius idea wasn't working.

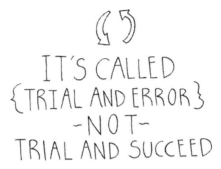

IT'S CALLED
{TRIAL AND ERROR}
-NOT-
TRIAL AND SUCCEED

The truth is, most people really don't want to exercise. They also don't know anything about you as a trainer; they just have these awful perceptions that they will be turning up for an hour of absolute torture from some muscle-bound idiot who can barely string a sentence together. How is this a prize? In their eyes it's clearly a punishment!

It took me a long time to realise that if I was going to stick with this idea then I really had to go all out with the prize and get people really excited about winning it.

Remember the early chapters that discussed how to "wow them", and the real price of advertising? I incorporated both of these ideas into my Big Give-Away idea and the results were massively different. So if you want to look great at a charity event and bring in clients for life then follow this protocol:

1. Meet with the event organiser.
2. Tell them you would like to offer them a prize for their charity event.
3. Explain that you would like to give them a voucher for six Personal Training sessions at your studio.
4. Tell them the value of this prize e.g. £300.
5. Wait for them to be amazed at your generosity.
6. Tell them that you have conditions:

1. This is advertised as the top prize.
2. There needs to be an explanation that you will offer a bespoke training package to the winner.
3. Request that you receive the winner's contact details once the prize has been given.
4. You put an expiry date on the voucher.

Why all these conditions?

1. You want to build excitement and get everyone at the event to see who you are and what you have given.
2. You make it clear that this is definitely a prize and not a punishment.
3. You speak to the winner to congratulate them, answer any questions they may have, reassure them that they will be looked after and then you book them in for the first session.

But six sessions is a lot to give away?!...

Here's the bit where you need to be clever. This is going to be a big investment of your time so you want to make sure you're working with a client who really wants to be there. I would suggest that you have an expiry time of six weeks after their first session and that their first session has to be booked within a month of winning the prize.

If they're not really into it then you won't hear from them again, and if they don't really want to stick to a programme then they'll find excuses not to turn up to sessions during those six weeks. You've just got to protect yourself from getting a call from someone a year after the event wanting to book one session per month for the next ten months and rearranging each one of them. Yes I've had one of those clients in the past as well and I dreaded every single session with her! Another mistake I've learnt from over time!

Get the right client, do your thing, get great results for them, build their trust and when the final session comes around they will really see the value in continuing to work with you and tell their friends about you as well. It really is a great way of marketing your business, getting new clients and feeling great about yourself at the same time!

After ten years in business I no longer personally deliver any of these sessions myself but instead give this job to the newest recruit on my team. The prize winner is none the wiser and it's a great way of getting my new trainer busy, and ensuring that they are implementing all of the coaching techniques and clients for life advice I have given to them.

CHAPTER 12
WIN THE OSCAR

HAVE YOU EVER left the cinema and been blown away by the performance of your favourite actor in their latest film, or left the theatre in awe of an incredible performance by someone you haven't even heard of?

What you may not have thought about is the fact that your favourite film actor has probably delivered fifty takes (often at their own request) of many of those scenes in that movie in order to blow you away. Or the fact that the amazing young actor you hadn't previously heard of delivers a perfect performance like that night after night – for years!

It all seems so effortless, but an actor knows that when the curtain goes up or the camera starts rolling, it's show time and they have to deliver the performance of their life, every time!

They know that they are in a very privileged position, doing something that they've dreamed of doing for years, and that they want to be able to keep doing this for the rest of their lives. It means everything to them and that's why they have to deliver, not for the people that are paying to watch them, but for themselves.

So ask yourself the question: what kind of performance do you deliver when the curtain goes up and the camera starts rolling in your line of work?

If you're going to be successful in this industry, then you need to be a great actor!

You're going to work long hours – very long hours, you're going to have clients who take their bad day out on you, you're going to have cash flow issues, you're going to get ill and you're going to have days when things just don't go your way.

You just need to leave this at the door each and every day.

When your paying client turns up, you need to bring your "A" game.

If you're going to be a successful personal trainer then you need to be a great actor. When the curtain goes up, slap on your makeup and your winning smile and get out there and deliver!

Clients are paying you to feel great about themselves; they don't want to hear about your sore throat or your argument with your girlfriend that morning. They need an hour that is all about them. They need an hour of your time that is dedicated to their needs. You may feel that you have built strong relationships over time with your clients and that they are really interested in hearing about your car breaking down AGAIN! Believe me, they don't!

It makes me laugh when I hear trainers say, "I have such a great relationship with my client, we talk about everything, and they are so good at giving me advice on life".... and then the client leaves! Guess what? Of course they enjoyed getting to know you, building a relationship and even hearing some of your stories, but later on they realised the sessions were no longer about them. They were paying you to be their counsellor, not getting what they wanted from the relationship and eventually had enough!

Clients need to be listened to; they need to be the main focus of your attention for the whole session and they need to leave the session feeling great about themselves after spending an hour with you, not desperate to get away from you and bored to tears of your depressing stories.

Always remember that you are there for the client, not the other way around. Remember you have two ears and one mouth, and listen twice as much as you talk to your clients. Become a great actor, leave your baggage at the door, be positive and deliver an award-winning performance – every time!

CHAPTER 13
THE BREAK-UP

LIKE ANY RELATIONSHIP, there comes a time when things may not be going quite to plan. It's inevitable that you probably won't see eye to eye all of the time with all of your clients and that they will do things every now and then that will upset you, annoy you, leave you feeling disappointed or just really piss you off!

The easiest thing would be to just walk away from any situation that doesn't go your way, but like any relationship, you need to assess the situation before you make any big decisions...

Is there more you could do?

Are you communicating effectively?

Are you seeing the world through their eyes?

Are you working hard to build their trust?

Are you going the extra mile?

OK, this bit is turning into the proper relationship advice section! Maybe I should think about that for my next book...

However, if the answer to all of the above questions is YES and you really feel as though you've done all you can to make things work then it's probably time to let go of that client.

If you find that every session is a constant battle then you need to break up.

If you find that you are dreading seeing a particular client then you need to break up.

Or if you think that you are not able to offer a client the best possible service or that your skillset just doesn't match their needs – then you need to break up.

But, like with any break-up, there is a right way and a wrong way to go about doing it

A number of years ago I had a client who was very difficult to work with. Her husband was paying for her training sessions and it was obvious from the start that she was resentfully turning up for him and not for herself. She really didn't want to come to the gym and she really didn't want to change.

I saw this very early on and I worked really hard to build trust with her, to find some common ground, and to have some fun with the training sessions. Initially we got on well; I really wanted to change her outlook, we built a good relationship, the conversation flowed and I thought she was a lovely lady but then the cracks started to form…

Her goal was to lose two stone and so I made it a habit to set her some simple nutritional goals each week. I would tell her that she could easily reach her target weight if she just made a few changes to her nutrition and lifestyle.

We would discuss cutting out alcohol and she would turn up the following week with an article from the Daily Mail that discussed the health benefits of red wine.

We would set a goal of reducing her sugar intake and she would find a study outlining why chocolate was a superfood.

I would tell her to drink more water and she would tell me about an article she had seen where someone had died from drinking too much water!

I would ask her to walk her dog every day and she would tell me I'd caused her knee pain.

The list goes on and on…Everything became such a battle but I didn't want to give up. Every week I prepared myself to be in a really positive mood for when she turned up but within minutes my optimism had turned to despair.

The traffic was terrible.

She wasn't able to park.

She proudly told me she hadn't done any homework since I last saw her.

And then if she had a newspaper clipping in her hand I knew I was going to struggle not to kill her!

I put up with this again for a few weeks but then after one really bad session I realised that not only was it affecting my mood during the session with her, but it was affecting my mood in the sessions beforehand and afterwards as well.

These other two clients that I saw before and after her were two of my favourite people, but I was unable to give much to the session before because of the dread that filled me prior to her session, and I was unable to really focus on the session after because I just felt absolutely shattered. Something had to change.

DON'T CLING
TO A MISTAKE
JUST BECAUSE
~YOU SPENT~
A LOT OF TIME
MAKING IT

These things are usually best done face to face but I didn't want to wait. I picked up the phone that evening after a particularly bad session and I told her that I could see that she really wasn't enjoying her sessions with me. I told her that I was there to support her but I didn't want to argue with her every week. I said that it was obvious she wasn't enjoying the sessions or getting anything out of them and I informed her that I wasn't either and therefore, I thought it was best if we stopped the training sessions with immediate effect.

The next day, I followed that up with a letter in which I thanked her for working with me for the last few months, wished her all the best for the future and suggested two other local trainers who I thought would be a better fit for her.

It was a nice break up!

There were no dramas, no arguing, no shouting and no tears.

We both went our separate ways and the best thing was that she ended up going with a trainer I suggested who I thought was a real pain in the arse! They were a perfect match; I couldn't be happier to see them together!

Now you may be reading this story thinking that I've given up on someone who really needed my help. I did think this myself briefly but then you have to look at the bigger picture.

You can't help people who don't want to help themselves.

Remember you have your own business and you choose who you work with.

Life is too short to spend time with people who make you unhappy.

Just simply remember that the longer you spend time with clients who you don't like, that you just can't help and that drain the life out of you, the less time you have to spend with amazing people who can really lift you, inspire you and allow you to be more, do more and give more.

There's a famous quote by the author and motivational speaker Jim Rohn that states: "You are the average of the five people you spend the most time with."

If you spend too much time with negative people who bring you down then you will inevitably end up that way. If you want to be positive, empowering and successful, spend time with people who make you feel that way!

You need to always look at yourself first and work out if there is anything that you can do to improve the relationships you have with your clients. If you've done all you can then cut the cord and set them free! Once you make the first decision I guarantee you won't regret it.

THE CLIENT AUDIT

I want you to make a list of all of your current clients and then place them into one of three groups:

1. The Favourites List – The clients who you really enjoy seeing. The clients who really value your time and experience, they follow your advice, give everything in their training sessions and you really enjoy their company. These are the type of clients that you would train for free!

2. The Improve List – The clients you have an up and down relationship with. You enjoy training them most of the time but you just need a bit more from them. You struggle a bit with conversation and the sessions drag slightly. They have the potential to join the favourites list but this will take some work on your behalf and theirs.

3. The Remove List – These are the clients who keep you awake at night dreading the next session. They drain the life out of you, they don't put in the work during your sessions and the conversation is painful. The only time they bring a smile to your face is when they cancel a session. They HAVE to go!

When you start out as a personal trainer any client with a wallet and a pulse is perfect for you! You are new to the game and so the fact that someone believes in you enough to pay for your services is a huge boost for you.

At this time I really believe it's great to be a jack of all trades and to work with clients of all ages and abilities and work out the type of client that you really want to train. When you're clear on who you are as a trainer, what you want to do with your business and WHY you want to do it, then it's your mission to find the type of client who fits your needs.

Learn from my experience. Be clear on the type of person that you really want to work with and be able to spot the type of person that you just can't help.

THE FILTER

Go out in any city centre on a Friday or Saturday night and you'll see queues of people outside every bar or nightclub. The better the venue, the bigger the queue and the bigger the queue, the more difficult it is to get in.

Outside each of these places is usually a couple of bouncers and a little velvet rope. If your face doesn't fit, if you're not wearing the right clothes or if these people decide that you're just not the right type of person for that establishment then you ain't getting in!

Can you put this type of filter into your business?

If anyone can easily get into a nightclub then it's probably not the best place to go. The wrong types of people will be attracted to this venue and as a result there is usually trouble around these places.

If you're INCLUSIVE of everyone then it actually loses appeal for some. If you're EXCLUSIVE then you are able to create more of a draw for clients. INCLUDING anyone with a wallet and a pulse will guarantee you troubles further down the line. EXCLUDING people that you know won't be a good fit at the start guarantees you will be working with great clients ALL of the time.

How do you do this?

Be clear at the start about what you expect from clients who want to work with you.

I decided that my ideal client would always have these four traits if they were going to be allowed into my EXCLUSIVE training club:

1. Positive: You will never get a positive result with a negative mind.

2. Hard working: Willing to give everything in each session and take responsibility for their results.

3. Committed: Punctual, focused and willing to see things through despite any setbacks that may arise.

4. Fun: Able to see the funny side of things and not take life too seriously.

If a client has all of these traits then I know I will enjoy the journey with them, I know I will get results with them, I know we will have fun along the way and that I will be able to make them "clients for life".

Before any of my team starts working with a client in my business we invite them in for a free consultation. Everyone loves something for free so this will all be viewed in a positive light by your potential clients. You explain to them that it is an opportunity for them to meet with you and other members of your team, look at your training studio and discuss exactly what they want to achieve from working with you.

What you don't say to them is that it's also an opportunity for you to assess whether they are going to pass the velvet rope and get into your exclusive club!

If they are negative, lazy, turn up late and the 30 minute consultation drags do you think they're going to be a great fit for you? I am a big believer in first impressions and going with your gut feeling. After working in the industry for 20 years I also think I'm now a good judge of determining which clients will be great to work with and who will be really hard work.

If I sense that certain clients aren't going to be a good fit then I make it more difficult for them to work with me.

I get them to do homework before they even start training with me by giving them a food diary to complete, for example.

I tell them that I can't see them at their ideal time and see if they are prepared to adjust their commitments to train with me.

I tell them stories of other clients' achievements but outline how hard they have had to work to achieve those results.

And I tell them that I'm not sure if they are ready to work with us at this stage and that I don't want them to waste their money if I don't believe they will be able to achieve the results that we really want for them.

My goal is to put them off. If they don't match my criteria then I don't want them to waste their money and blame me for not getting the results they came in for. I also don't want any of my coaches to have to work with clients who they are going to want to break up with a few weeks down the line. It's best for both parties that the break-up happens before we even get started!

Funnily enough, this process can often have a positive outcome. The client recognises that if they are going to get into this "Exclusive Club" then they need to follow the rules. All of a sudden they become a bit more POSITIVE about training. They realise that they are prepared to be HARD WORKING throughout the process, they tell you how COMMITTED they will be towards their goal and the whole experience becomes FUN.

Now we have a potential client for life!

Be exclusive. Determine exactly what types of clients you want to work with, what traits you want to see in these people, what you're prepared to compromise on and what you just won't accept. Be clear from the outset that you require a certain level of commitment. Once you've allowed people into your club, follow the processes outlined in this book and continue to wow them over and over again.

CHAPTER 14
BE DIFFERENT

AS I'VE ALREADY stated, you need to stand out from the crowd. Don't be like everyone else – anyone can call themselves a personal trainer – don't follow the crowd, but create a new position for yourself.

I have a velvet rope around my business and I am very selective over who I let into my team; as a result I am fortunate enough to have some of the most talented coaches in the business working at All About You. They are very highly qualified, very hard working, very positive people that I enjoy spending time with. They create excellent programmes that achieve fantastic results, they deliver five star service and as a result they are all trusted trainers that have clients for life.

They deliver something that is so much more powerful than just training. They all continue to learn more and give more to the clients each and every week and they all know that they are part of a special team. They aren't arrogant, but they know they are better than a run-of-the-mill trainer and they work for a business that is different to your run-of-the-mill gym, and they want everyone to know that.

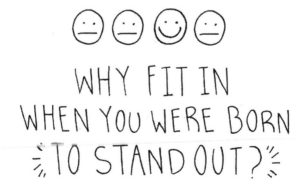

Embrace your own uniqueness: let's face it, you get up at 5am, you wear a tracksuit to work, you probably consume more broccoli in a week than an average family of four eats in a year, you're determined, you break the rules and you do things your own way. You're different, so tell everyone.

If you specialise in getting post-natal mums back to their pre-baby weight, then tell everyone that!

Likewise, if you have a special talent for fixing injuries, stripping fat or creating athletic physiques then tell everyone about it.

Often the most talented coaches have come from failed previous careers. Failed sportsmen and failed performers are very commonly drawn to the health and fitness world. Nowadays it is also very common to see a number of people who have escaped the rat race in order to pursue a career where they can take care of themselves a lot more. This journey often leads them back into the corporate world, where they can share their story of how the demands of their job nearly broke them but now they want to lead by example.

Everyone has a unique story and a very individual skillset. Find yours and then incorporate that into the work you do.

I am a failed sportsman who was injured time and time again when I was younger, and it sparked an interest in human anatomy and movement. It led me to working with some of the best osteopaths, physiotherapists and surgeons in the country and to creating my own approach to corrective exercise.

Find your uniqueness and tell your own story; it will give you so much clarity and enable you to work out the type of client you really want to work with and also, more importantly, enable you to realise why you do what you do.

CHAPTER 15
DON'T GIVE UP

BUILDING A BUSINESS isn't going to be an easy ride. In fact, at times it's going to be really tough: you're probably going to fall out with friends, family and your partner because they just won't understand why you need to work so hard. It takes a certain person to even consider setting up a business and most people just aren't built that way!

The truth is that around 50% of businesses will fail within the first five years of operating and around 70% of businesses never make it to ten years.

You're going to get uncomfortable on your business journey, very uncomfortable at times, you're going to have to take a lot of risks, make a lot of sacrifices and learn to function on very little sleep!

So you need to have a really clear vision of what you aim to achieve and know exactly WHY you're doing what you're doing.

WHEN THINGS GO WRONG
AS THEY SOMETIMES WILL,
WHEN THE ROAD YOU'RE TRUDGING
SEEMS ALL UPHILL,
WHEN THE FUNDS ARE LOW
AND THE DEBTS ARE HIGH
AND YOU WANT TO SMILE,
BUT HAVE TO SIGH.
WHEN CARE IS PRESSING
YOU DOWN A BIT...
REST IF YOU MUST
BUT DO NOT QUIT

If you've decided to set up your own business, then you're not normal! Normal people quit when things get slightly uncomfortable; entrepreneurs know that the magic happens when they get really uncomfortable!

If you find yourself in a bit of trouble once your business is up and running then you're going to have to get even more uncomfortable to resolve these issues. When I lost over £100,000 from a bad business decision I made several years ago, my plan involved sleeping at my gym for four months. It was a terrible plan but I knew it would make me uncomfortable enough to force me to make things happen.

Most people give up on their dreams too easily and then live with the regret of what might have been. If you have a dream then do everything you can to make it a reality, and when you look back in the years to come it will be even more special, trust me!

If you know WHY you are building your business, why you want to make a difference to the world and how your contribution is going to create a positive effect on the people that you work with – and more importantly create a positive change in your own life and of those closest to you – then you will find that your journey becomes a lot easier. You bounce out of bed when that alarm goes off, you brush off any negative comments that come your way, you embrace the challenges that inevitably fall at your door and you will grow as a person as a result of these events.

I guarantee there will be many occasions when you will question what you do and wonder if it is all really worthwhile. If you don't have that clear goal fixed in your mind, if that vision of who you will become, what you will achieve and how you will create a positive impact is not clear enough for you, then failure is inevitable. But, if you can clearly determine your purpose and set out day after day to achieve your dream I promise the setbacks will be temporary and the success will be even sweeter!

A LITTLE SIDE NOTE

Sleeping in your gym for four months does not deserve any praise. I am not proud in any way of that part of my life. It was a decision that I made at that time because as a single man with no one depending upon me, it was something that I believed was worth doing in order to save the only thing that meant anything to me at that time. As a result of that action my business has gone on to achieve so much more and so I can look back now and say that I guess it was worthwhile for me.

However, this may not be the case for you. If things are going unbelievably badly for you then ignore the title of this chapter! Throw the towel in and move on with your life. You gave it a go but for whatever reason things just haven't worked out. It takes real courage to walk away from something that is no longer serving you.

Businesses unfortunately close every day; often simple mismanagement on the part of the owner has fatal consequences. However, numerous businesses close their doors for reasons out of the owner's hands. Political, economic and social changes take place that impact heavily on a number of businesses and the owners simply cannot continue.

The tough lesson to learn is that your chances of succeeding without at least a few hiccups along the way are pretty slim. Be sure you always stay focused on the fact that your work is just simply what you do, and make sure it doesn't completely define you as a person. If it isn't working out, walk away; if it is making you unwell, walk away; if it is ruining your relationships with the people closest to you then walk away. Close that door and find a new one to open.

RE-CAP AND PUT IT INTO ACTION

You've read a number of ideas on what needs to be done to create clients for life; now it's time to go over a few of the important points and really put it all into action. It's easy to read through the chapters in this book, to scribble down some notes and create a plan for success. None of this means anything until you actually put that plan into action!

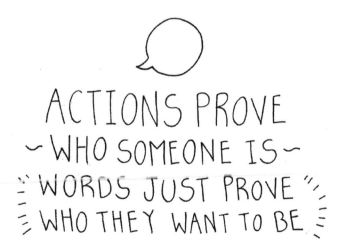

CHAPTER 16
THE IMPORTANCE OF COMMUNICATION

IN THIS DAY and age there is no excuse for not being able to contact someone. We are bombarded all day with calls, texts, emails, tweets, and social media updates and messages.

The key to building relationships with your clients and communicating effectively with them is to know when to contact them, and in what way you should contact them.

You need to be consistent with your communication. Just calling a client when they owe you money is not a good way to build a relationship; a call out of the blue to check on their training or just to see how they're doing is a great way to build great relationships with your clients.

As I mentioned previously I don't spend a huge amount of money on marketing my business, but I do invest in retaining my clients. Each of my trainers invests a lot of time on the phone in order to maintain regular contact with each client, and we have systems in place to improve those relationships further.

One of the keys to becoming a trusted trainercl is the element of surprise.

Doing something out of the blue makes a client think that you really care for them. If you've got systems in place you may not know that these gestures have even been made.

Earlier this week a client at the studio came up to me and thanked me for his birthday card and massage voucher, and said that it was the best present he received! It turns out he had just injured himself playing football and was really in need of a treatment.

I obviously said I hoped he had a great day and really enjoyed his massage, but had absolutely no idea it was his birthday as my admin assistant takes care of that side of the business.

Make yourself part of their life

One of the biggest mistakes trainers make with their clients is to change the times and days they see their clients. Unless they have a very good reason for constantly changing their time don't let this happen.

Firstly you will create more of a routine to your own life and secondly you become part of your client's life – they know that on a Wednesday at 9am they are coming to see you every week!

Now, here is the big tip – if for whatever reason you don't see them one Wednesday morning at 9am, contact them. If they're on holiday, email them to wish them a great time or check they are following the training programme you wrote for them. (Maybe not at 9am while they're on holiday but at some point during the day!)

It will take a few seconds but it will keep you in that client's mind for a long time and I guarantee they'll be back in the following week. Email is always best in this situation because your client will choose to look at it; a call or a text may be too invasive during some precious time away.

Most clients drop off from training because of a lack of communication. They leave it a while after a holiday break, the trainer forgets to call or can't be bothered to call, and it stays that way for so long both of them are too embarrassed to make contact again.

It takes a few seconds to send a text message. A few minutes to make a call – man up and do it! It's a hell of a lot easier than marketing for new clients every week!

Have you ever found it's difficult to get a client to come back into a routine, or have you dreaded a conversation with someone because you know you've not spoken to them for a while?

A two-second text can be enough to keep a client training with you, get them back training with you after a holiday and also get them telling their friends about you – probably adding up to a few thousand pounds a year in your back pocket!

Don't give up on clients too easily. Contacting them again is not pestering them; just value what you do and know that you are delivering a fantastic service that will really improve your credentials as a trusted trainer' – you're doing them a disservice if you don't call them again!

That phone call could also potentially be worth thousands of pounds to you and could also allow your client to drop a dress size and look and feel amazing about themselves in just a few weeks – Just Do It!

CHAPTER 17
THE POWER OF PROBLEMS

IF THERE IS one thing I can guarantee for your business, it's that you will face problems. Things won't quite turn out as you had planned, people will let you down and various challenging scenarios will present themselves to you throughout your journey. When problems arise, always see them as an opportunity to show your ability to lead or your ability to crumble.

We have all CHOSEN to be self-employed. We've decided not to take the easy route of a comfortable salary and a steady 9-5. We've done this because we're all passionate people, we want to follow our passion every day and be the masters of our own destiny – but this isn't always easy.

I had a realisation earlier this year that there will NEVER be a perfect day when you run your own business!

The day I walk into All About You and every client loves me, every trainer turns up early, dressed immaculately and full of enthusiasm, every payment is received on time, every competitor goes out of business and a nice warm cup of coffee is waiting for me on the front desk is the day I have died!

I've realised that wishing for "just one day where everything can run smoothly" is a waste of my time!

The truth is: there will ALWAYS be problems. That's just part of business and of life.

The real test is how you deal with the problems – this is what sets you apart from everyone else.

If you are GREAT at what you do then you solve problems better than anyone else.

In the same way that solving your client's health and fitness problems in a better way than anyone else makes you great at what you do!

If clients didn't have any problems then YOU wouldn't have a job.

That's why problems are GREAT: because they give us all a chance to show how GREAT WE ARE!

This doesn't mean that creating more problems for yourself will make you happy by the way!

It means that you should embrace the problems that come your way and see them as an opportunity to grow – because if you're not growing anywhere, you're not going anywhere.

CHAPTER 18
BE INTERESTING AND INTERESTED

HAIRDRESSER SYNDROME

"**G**OING ANYWHERE NICE on your holidays?"

"What are you doing at the weekend?"

Why do most trainers have no conversation except the crap chat you'd get from a 17-year-old trainee?

If you aren't interesting or interested in the session, how the hell do you expect your clients to be?

Get some energy!

Get some passion and enthusiasm for what you do!

Learn more, have the answer to your client's problems and make sure that you have some really interesting things to say and show that you are interested in your client.

Become more emotionally intelligent and learn how to strike up intelligent conversation with all types of people.

Get some energy

A favourite quote of mine:

IF YOU ARE NOT FIRED WITH ENTHUSIASM YOU'LL BE FIRED WITH ENTHUSIASM!

It may sound a bit harsh but seriously, remember WHY you are doing what you're doing.

If your client really wanted to train then they wouldn't need you. If they loved exercise as much as you then they'd do it on their own. If they were as confident as you in a gym environment then you would be out of a job.

It's absolutely essential that you are fired with enthusiasm for every single client that you see!

I'm sure you know this, so why aren't you willing to go all out to deliver the best possible experience for your client EVERY SINGLE TIME? This is what pisses me off more than anything about other personal trainers…

Don't be a rep counter!

You're better than that. You're a coach, not a counter. You've read the books, you've gone on the courses, you live and breathe fitness, and you need to bring it all together with a personality that inspires.

Many trainers will read this book and completely disagree with what I have to say. I won't be losing any sleep because of that. Like I said, this book isn't based on a few ideas that have been thrown together; this is based on my own real life experiences from someone who has been in the health and fitness industry for twenty years.

M,any trainers may see things in a completely different way, but many trainers in the industry don't last more than a few years! Many trainers in the industry will always work for someone else, many trainers in the industry won't earn enough money to pay their bills and sadly, many trainers in the industry won't have the ability to actually strike up conversation and build relationships with people.

They have a personality bypass, and they really believe that they're not doing their job if they don't beast and abuse their clients for the whole time they are with them. You can still push your clients, get great results and give them an enjoyable experience at the same time.

As a coach you learn the importance of good form, the need for good posture, the necessity for appropriate cueing, the requirements for explaining sets, reps, rest periods and tempo, you recognise the importance of building a relationship with each client and most importantly showing off these skills!

But you still stand there and count?!

You have the ability to spot mistakes,

The knowledge to correct poor posture,

The experience to explain how movements should be correctly performed,

The talent to design great programmes and the ability to wow your client so that they choose to come back to you because they actually like you...

But you still just stand there and count?!!

Think about it!

What are you there for?

To encourage or to count?

To correct or to shout out numbers?

To advise or to go through the motions?

To inspire or to bore?

Ask yourself again, what would a £100-per-hour trainer do, how would they act, and what would they talk about?

Trust me; your client doesn't want to hand over their hard-earned cash to hear you count to ten over and over for an hour!

I'm sure you can feel that it's a real pet hate of mine. Anyone can stand there and count, but an expert coach with clients for life will always find ways to inspire their clients to achieve more and bring enjoyment to their sessions.

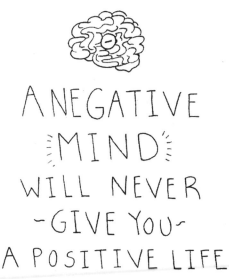

A NEGATIVE MIND WILL NEVER -GIVE YOU- A POSITIVE LIFE

Working as a health and fitness professional is one of the best jobs that anyone can do. Every day you get to do something that you love, show that passion and really make a positive impact on the lives of the clients who you work with.

Stop seeing it as a hassle to spend time with certain clients. Stop looking bored to tears during these sessions; if you're just going through the motions with your clients do you really think they'll want to come back to work with you?

Do yourself a favour and stop putting yourself through these types of sessions. Either stop seeing the client because they are that painful to work with, or stop doing the job, because you're clearly not up to it.

Rant over!

CHAPTER 19
HOW TO BE A GREAT TRAINER

THE SAD FACT is that most people don't last in the fitness industry for more than a few years. In fact 70% of trainers will quit within four years of qualifying, the main reasons being a lack of money, the inability to acquire new clients and having to work unsociable hours.

I don't want this to happen to you. You're in this industry because you're passionate about your own health and fitness and you want to help others be passionate about theirs. It's a fantastic industry to be a part of, and incredibly rewarding to those who are prepared to do the hard work.

This little book will help you to build exceptional relationships with your clients; you just need to believe in yourself. Aim high: don't accept second best in any element of your life. Don't be part of that 70% statistic; there are plenty of people that are earning serious money from this industry and you can be one of them.

Money is always an important subject to address with every trainer who works within my business, and I am proud to be able to offer my team the ability to earn significantly higher salaries than 90% of the industry. The team are given support, structure and an individualised plan to work to, and an environment in which they can learn, grow and become the best that they can be.

Within my business there is always opportunity for trainers to earn more money from improving their skillset and increasing their prices, but I like to set them this challenge:

If you want to be a £100-per-hour trainer, start acting like one from day one.

Task:

Answer each of these questions and improve yourself as a trainer overnight:

What does a £100-per-hour trainer look like?

How does a £100-per-hour trainer act?

What do they think about?

What do they talk about?

What do they study and which books do they read?

How do they dress?

How do they keep their clients?

What kind of results do they get with their clients?

The key to keeping clients for life is to build a strong relationship, and the key to any relationship is to keep working at improving it. Answer these questions for yourself, believe in your own ability and I guarantee you won't be part of the industry drop-outs.

CHAPTER 20
WORKING ON YOU

THE KEY LESSON to take from this book is this: if you want to be successful in the health and fitness business then you have to be the best version of yourself. You need to look great, feel great, inspire people around you at every opportunity and be the type of person that you enjoy being around because let's face it, if you don't enjoy your own company how do you expect anyone else to?!

As soon as you stop making an effort and taking someone for granted the relationship is over.

Building a relationship with a client is just like building a relationship with a partner. You need to attract them, impress them, do what you promise you're going to do and then always leave them wanting more.

Don't wait for the next qualification, for another two years' experience or for permission from someone else… Decide NOW that you are going to be the best trainer that you can be and put on a great performance at every opportunity.

Fifteen ways to improve every training session you deliver:

1. **ARRIVING:** making sure you are in the moment and leaving whatever is going on in your world away from the session. Always arrive early; if you're on time then you're late! Be ready at least ten minutes before the agreed time, be prepared and relaxed and the session will go well. Be rushed, late and flustered and you can virtually guarantee the session won't be one of your best. We all have bad days from time to time but remember your client isn't paying to hear you moan about the parking ticket you picked up this morning or the row with your girlfriend last night. Leave your problems at the door, focus on your client, give them a great session and BOTH of you will feel great at the end of it.

2. **SMILE:** not just at your client but at everyone who comes through the door; they could be your next client. Get in the habit of having a smile on your face most of the day; it's pretty tough to be in a bad mood with a smile on your face!

Maybe I'm a bit cynical after working in London for 15 years where a lot of people have forgotten what smiling feels like! It takes minimal effort and it costs nothing, but it makes you a better person to be around and makes you feel better. If you're a positive, fun person to be around clients will be drawn to you.

3. **SESSION TIME:** if your client is late for a genuine reason there is no need to get stressed; just work for the allotted time. Determine your own approach to clients turning up late, but remember it's their problem, not yours. If there is a genuine reason then just move on, but if it happens again it should be your responsibility to address this issue. A client that consistently turns up late will not achieve the results they want and will be a poor advert for your business.

4. **ESTABLISH HABITS:** be aware of what you establish – get payments on time and try and keep to your diary – you run your diary, not your clients. Run your "personal training business" as a business! Being self-employed in the health and fitness industry means that your working week will not be 9-5. There will be early starts, late nights and weekend work. Whatever hours you do, create a schedule, be consistent each week with all of your habits and life will be easy.

5. **FOCUS:** fully focus on what is happening in front of you. If a client is paying you good money they deserve your full attention during their time. Block out other people training around you and stop day-dreaming about what you're getting up to at the weekend. That person you are training is the ONLY person that matters for the next hour!

6. **PROFESSIONAL:** the more professional you are the more you can earn; it's that simple! Probably the single, biggest mistake most personal trainers make is a lack of professionalism. Grade yourself out of 10 on the following: your appearance, your uniform, your business cards, your website, your knowledge, the quality of your sessions, your income and your job satisfaction. Improve all of these and clients will be drawn to you and have no reason to leave.

7. **YOU or THEM:** My business is called All About You, and I have a lovely saying that I share with my trainers when they piss me off: "The You in All About You isn't YOU!" Every client that comes through the door is the YOU in All

About You. Remember that a PT session is all about the client. That doesn't mean you give them an easy session because that's what they want! You give them a programme designed to their specific needs and have a really positive effect on their day. Put the client's needs ahead of yours and recognise that you have the ability to make every person you come in contact with feel better about themselves. That's really powerful, and in turn, I guarantee you'll feel pretty good about yourself as a result!

8. **THE SPACE:** the space you work in defines you and every person who trains with you in it. Do you want people to think you're dirty, disorganised and falling apart?! YOU need to take responsibility for it, keep it clean and leave it as you wish to find it. Even if your space is your shed at the bottom of your garden, take pride in that space and in everything that you do.

9. **GRATITUDE:** remember to say thank you to all who work with you. People don't hear those words enough. This simple act of showing your clients that you really appreciate them choosing to work with you will go a lot further than you can imagine.

10. **CHOICES:** if you are having a bad day – remind yourself that you chose to do this job. A lot of the time this may involve making others feel better about themselves and putting yourself last. Deal with it! A successful business will ultimately make you a lot happier.

11. **PAYMENTS:** a number of trainers have issues with asking for money. Don't be like this. You provide a service and this needs to be paid for. Remember this simple process of give and take creates balance. Decide that you will be assertive around this type of issue and both you and your client will benefit from this.

12. **SKILLS:** work to your strengths and build a team to support you. Can someone else offer a better service with massage, nutrition or injury rehabilitation? Create your own "Team" to support you and offer an improved service to your clients.

13. **ATMOSPHERE:** create an atmosphere for the cross-section of clients – be aware of what music is playing on the sound system. Coming to the gym is a time for the client to feel good; if you have a sixty-year-old lady does she really want to listen to your hip hop album? Ensure that you always maintain good relationships with those that you work with. Any tension between you and

other trainers will be obvious to see and make your clients feel uncomfortable. You don't need to be best friends with everyone; you just need to keep things amicable to maintain a positive working environment.

14. **FLEXIBLE:** make sure that you are flexible with all the other trainers in the space and always be flexible with the client's needs. Average trainers fail every time with this. Great trainers will always adapt to any situation.

15. **TRANSITION:** in an ideal world leave at least fifteen minutes between client sessions. This gives you the time to clear your mind, grab something to eat, have a toilet visit, respond to any phone messages and get your game face on for your next client. Answer this question: if you have five sessions back-to-back can the person coming in for session five really expect to receive five star service?!

CHAPTER 21
RAISING THE BAR

THE REAL SECRET to keeping your clients for life and in turn not only transforming your business, but also your life, is to really raise the bar with every interaction and build relationships with people that go way above the typical client-trainer roles.

The whole purpose of me writing this book was to document a process for myself that would allow me to not only build a business that can thrive for years to come, but also to build a life for myself that can continually give me new and exciting experiences. It is my hope that by reading this book you will be able to achieve the same for yourself.

As I stated in the opening chapter, life is all about the people who you meet and the opportunities that you create with them. It is my belief that opportunities are everywhere; the problem is that people simply don't manage these opportunities properly.

They either don't see the opportunity even when it's staring them in the face, or worse, they push too much for it and scare it away.

The night I won an award for my business I shared a few images from the evening on social media. The next morning when I checked my phone there were some great messages from friends and colleagues who were genuinely pleased for my success.

I also had messages from a load of people within the fitness industry who had contacted me to push their crappy products onto my clients. I knew all of these people but I didn't know anything about their products, and if they had actually taken the time to speak to me about this they would have found out that I don't push crappy products onto my clients. I don't see any benefit in trying to sell rubbish I don't believe in to my clients just so that I can take an extra fiver off them!

These guys had witnessed my success and then simply seen an opportunity for themselves. There was no attempt to "Date me", wow me or provide me with a solution that could really benefit my life and that of my clients. They went straight for the money shot and immediately lost my attention. If that is their approach with everyone then I'm pretty confident that things aren't going to work out that well for them.

You have to do the ground work, you have to put in the time to earn trust and then you need to keep over-delivering. In my opinion this is the only way to build amazing relationships. We live in a world that constantly seeks instant gratification and quick-fix solutions to everything in life. The reality is it often takes most people ten years to become an overnight success!

The image below is a favourite of mine and perfectly illustrates the different stages of loyalty with clients as you take them on a journey through your business.

It is your duty as a great business owner to take as many people as far up the ladder of loyalty as you can. In doing so amazing things will start to happen for you and your business. Let me explain…

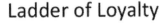

Ladder of Loyalty

- **Partner:** Someone who has the relationship of partner with you.
- **Advocate:** Someone who actively recommends you to others, who does your marketing for you.
- **Supporter:** Someone who likes your organisation, but only supports you passively.
- **Client:** Someone who has done business with you on a repeat basis but may be negative, or at best neutral, towards your organisation.
- **Purchaser:** Someone who has done business just once with your organisation.
- **Prospect:** Someone whom you believe may be persuaded to do business with you.

Source: Christopher, Payne & Ballantyne, Relationship Marketing

PROSPECT

Every person who ever emails you, picks up the phone to enquire about your business or actually comes into your facility for a consultation with you could be a potential game changer in your business. Remember this when you decide to judge someone by the way that they look, what they do for a living or even their name. It may sound ridiculous but you could be throwing away incredible opportunities before they even have a chance to show up. You want a business that gives you a great life? Then treat every meeting with a new prospect like a potentially life-changing experience – because one day one of them will be!

PURCHASER

Let's be brutally honest here. If you have Purchasers in your business then you have failed my friend. The definition of a Purchaser is someone who does business with you once and so if you're going to build a successful business the first thing you need to do is to make sure you find clients who are going to stick around for more than one session.

As we've discussed throughout this book, you don't need to appeal to everyone. In fact trying to be everything to everyone is a sure fire way to leave you feeling stressed and frustrated. Just get clear on exactly what your ideal client looks like, determine exactly what they require from you and then keep over-delivering.

CLIENT

This should now be the minimum standard that you are aiming for with every person that comes into your business. If you can achieve this then you will have a reasonably successful business. It won't be easy; you will still have to work very hard at it, but it should give you a great sense of satisfaction and achievement that you have created a business that works for you.

If you are happy with this, keep doing what you're doing. A huge number of businesses will remain in this position for years with reasonable success and a number of businesses can thrive in this position if there is no competition in the area.

The danger of this type of business is that whilst the owner has a good relationship with his clients it may not strong enough. If an identical business offering a higher level of service opened across the road then a business at this level could be lost almost overnight. That's why your goal HAS to be to raise the bar and aim for your clients to fall into the following categories…

SUPPORTER

This is the standard that you should now be aiming for with each person who comes into your business. They really like you, they really like what your business does and they will continue to support you. They just want to keep you as their little secret at this stage.

You've got to remember that not everyone is going to scream and shout about your business. If people are coming to you to change something about themselves then this is a very personal process, and the majority of people don't feel the need to post about every training session on social media or tell all of the mums in the coffee shop about you. The fact that they really like your business and will continue to support you may just be enough.

However, if you believe that you can always do more (and if you're still reading this far into the book then you certainly do by now) it is your responsibility now to look at each of your supporters and work out how you can serve each one of them at a higher level in order to take them further up the ladder.

ADVOCATE

These clients are worth their weight in gold. You only need a handful of these types of people to really explode your business. Whilst you still need to continue to look for better ways to serve your clients and supporters, you really need to go above and beyond for your advocates.

How do you reward them for the referrals that they pass to you? What do you do for them to celebrate their birthday? How do you surprise them with a random act to show them how important they are to you and your business?

The terrible thing is that some people don't even know that they have these types of clients within their business. If you know your business well enough then you should know where each of your clients comes from. If your answer is "word of mouth" then you need to find out whose words and whose mouth!

80% of your business will always come from 20% of your contacts. Find those 20% and give them more.

PARTNER

If you reach this level with your clients then not only are you doing a pretty amazing job with them but also, you're opening up the possibilities of taking your life and career to a whole new level.

Partnering with your clients will open up a number of doors for you and opportunities that you never realised were possible when you first started your business. You will realise that whilst having your own business, pursuing your own dream, being the master of your own destiny and living life by your rules is an amazing experience, your life and business can take a huge upturn when you partner with someone who's competing on a whole new level!

Here are just a few examples of the partnerships that I am currently embarking on with my business:

I have been able to demonstrate to a leading London physiotherapist that my business and my team are the best in London, and that by working with us he will be able to deliver more to his clients by offering excellent corrective exercise programmes, sports therapy and progressive strength and conditioning training. He agreed to bring his clinic into my business and the first client he brought through the doors was a premier league footballer!

One of my biggest advocates is a great old boy called Jack, who was kind enough to write a little testimonial for this book and also good enough to introduce me to a huge number of clients over the last ten years! One of these people was a property developer; his company creates unbelievable homes in the North London area and he has taken on some incredible projects over the last few years. He is a very busy guy and so it has been my goal to push him to achieve more physically during the good times and encourage rest, recovery, massage and good nutrition during his incredibly stressful times.

He has just finished a building project on one of the most exclusive roads in London. This development of 20 apartments that start at £6 million each has an on-site gym, 25-metre pool, sauna, steam room, treatment rooms and relaxation lounges, and he has given my company the contract to manage these facilities.

Another client is one of the most senior consultants in education in the country. He is known as a "super head" who is brought in to failing schools to address the underlying causes of failure, restructure the team, build morale and create a shared vision for the school to achieve success. Amongst his many roles is to organise conferences around the country to promote new ideas in education, and these events always have a strong emphasis on the health and wellbeing of the kids being taught and the adults teaching them.

He has trust and belief in my abilities and as a result I have been given the opportunity to speak at a number of these conferences. This has given me the opportunity to reach a new audience, develop new skills and get paid very well in the process.

Then there is the truly life-changing partnership I have developed in the last few years when I started to work with the head of a Formula

One Team six months prior to his wedding to his high profile partner. I did my thing, he looked great on his wedding day and not only have I continued to work one-to-one with him each week, but he has also brought me into the Formula One Team as a Human Performance Coach. It's a dream job for me and has opened up a new path in my career that wouldn't have been accessible to me without a partnership and relationship being formed.

So raise the bar in your life. Raise the bar with your own standards and expectations of yourself, raise the bar with the expectations of the colleagues and friends who you spend your time with. Raise the bar in the delivery of your sessions, and in every communication that you have with your clients. Raise the bar with your appearance, in your own fitness levels and raise the bar on what you really believe is possible in your career. A life-changing opportunity may only be one conversation away so be ready for it!

CHAPTER 22
YOUR TO-DO LIST

IT SHOULD BE your goal to continually work on three key areas on a consistent basis:
1. Improving you
2. Improving your client's experience
3. Improving your business as a whole.

Consistent improvements require consistent action. Below is a list of weekly, monthly, quarterly and yearly actions that you should aim to take in order to see great results in all three of these key areas.

WEEKLY
- Contact all of your clients to confirm their training session that week.
- Determine an opportunity to wow a client this week.
- Follow up and take action on the notes you made after last week's sessions.
- Take one client out for coffee.
- Introduce yourself to one new person or business.
- Send some business to someone local or spend money with them yourself.
- Take a walk on your local High Street just to say hello to people (trust me on this one!).
- Tell your story on social media.
- Read a book, listen to a podcast and find the time to study.
- Write a weekly report for yourself and determine what you can do next week to be even better. Start by answering these questions:
  What exciting things happened in my business this week? Who did I thank, compliment or praise this week? What mistakes did I make this week and how can I learn from them? What does my ideal day look like?

MONTHLY

- Go through your list of clients and write birthday cards for everyone celebrating this month.
- Write an inspiring and entertaining newsletter for all of your clients.
- Book each of your clients in for a monthly review of their training and set new goals.
- Contact two clients who you haven't seen for a while and encourage them to come back and train with you.
- Send a hand-written thank you card to a client. Thank them for referring a friend to you, for helping you out with something or just because you enjoy training them.
- Reward your client of the month. Celebrate the success of your hardest working client. At my studios they receive a massage, a voucher for a meal at a local restaurant and a trophy.
- Ask some of your clients to complete a survey for you. Ask for their suggestions on how you can improve your service to them.
- Write something. Write an article for one client, post on your blog, write for someone else or write a chapter of your own book; just get in the habit of writing each month.
- Take time out. Even if it's just a weekend away from work you need to make sure you practice what you preach. Rest, reflect and renew so you can give more to your clients next month.

QUARTERLY

- Set up a community event or involve yourself in something that is already going on locally.
- Produce reports for your clients to show them the results they have achieved.
- Produce a report for yourself to review what activities have worked well in your business in the last few months.
- Put your clients into groups. Who will you keep, who will you improve and who will you remove?
- Go on a course. Not online, not a home study course, get out there and meet like-minded people. Often great things will come from the connections you make as well as the knowledge you will gain.
- Are you on track? Where do you want to take your business? What actions do you need to take in the next three months to move things in the direction you want to go?

- Why are you getting up in the morning? Remember the big question – why do you do what you do? If you know your why you can deal with any how.

YEARLY

- How much money did you make? However passionate you are about what you do and however much you care about your clients, you need to make enough money to keep doing it, and if you've built a business then you need to make some serious money to justify the risk you have taken.
- Are you enjoying what you do? You can't live a life you love, if you're doing things you loathe. Make the changes that will allow you to love your business again.
- How can you improve you? Make a list for yourself, ask a friend or colleague how you can improve and get a trusted client to give you some brutally honest feedback.
- How can you improve your business? Design an anonymous survey and send it to your clients asking for their constructive criticism.
- How can you excite your clients about staying to work with you next year?
- What can you do differently to improve things for your clients and yourself?
- How can you reward your clients' loyalty next year?
- What sporting events and fitness challenges can you plan for next year?
- What social events can you plan for next year?
- How can you implement as many ideas from this book as possible next year?!

CHAPTER 23
BUILDING RELATIONSHIPS WITH ALL TYPES OF CLIENTS

NOW WE TURN to the truly actionable stuff. In this section I'm going to share a simple, step-by-step process to effectively manage the different types of clients that I've encountered in my career. As I've discussed in earlier chapters, your working relationship with a client can rapidly change from one week to the next. The key to success is in always being one step ahead, anticipating problems where possible, quickly adapting to unforeseen circumstances and offering possible solutions (or at least knowing where to look to find the solution).

Just when you think everything is going well with your client base, something will come along to burst your bubble. Changing, unpredictable circumstances are part of life and an ever-present feature of running a small business – so get used to it!

In the following sections of this chapter I will set out some special situations with certain types of client that I have encountered in my professional career to date. The basic principle that underpins each of them is that to be one of the best trainers in the world you must adopt a client-centred approach to your interactions and personalise your advice. In many cases, a personalised touch does not cost a significant amount of extra time or money but separates you from the hordes of other trainers just looking to "make a quick buck". In no particular order, here are some types of clients I have developed particular strategies for over the years:

THE EXPECTANT MOTHER

When a client tells you she is pregnant you should think positively! Bear in mind that you, as their trainer, will probably be one of the first to hear the news. At all costs, do not give the client any sense that you're disappointed at the prospect of losing their custom for a year or so.

This situation presents an amazing opportunity to provide advice and support at a critical time in a client's life, thereby strengthening the client relationship. Seen from their perspective, this is an amazing, life-changing event and they need all the professional wellness advice that they can get. It is key to show them you share in their joy and excitement and will be with them every step of the way.

Take note of the following steps when advising pregnant women to make the whole process a mutually positive experience:

Send your client an article outlining the benefits of exercising when pregnant (a sample can be found on my blog: davidosgathorp.com).

Send your client guidelines for exercising safely when pregnant to reassure them you know what you're doing and will look after them throughout their pregnancy, a time when their overall health and wellness are paramount.

Be understanding. Expect a pregnant woman to cancel sessions due to sickness, stress, tiredness and other concerns relating to their pregnancy. Show compassion and understanding throughout their pregnancy and they'll be keen to seek post-natal training advice.

During the pregnancy, consult with your client about what steps you can take together after their pregnancy to work towards the very common goal to "lose the baby weight". Your job at this stage with this type of client should be to get them excited and motivated about getting back into shape well, well before their waters break.

Remember to keep regular (I recommend weekly) contact with your client during periods when they are unable to train. This can be simple: for example, a short note by email or text message wishing them well or forwarding them a relevant article, such as those mentioned above, can be a very good way of keeping you front and centre of their minds for when they do eventually return to the gym floor.

Diarise a rough time with your client to begin their post-natal training programme (usually 6-8 weeks after the birth is a good time to start).

Don't pressure a new mother back into training; just tactfully let them know you are there for them when they feel ready to come back to the gym.

A simple tip but one that works wonders and not many trainers do: send them a greetings card congratulating them on the birth.

Depending on the level of familiarity between you, it may be appropriate to visit the client (and their new arrival!) in person, perhaps offering a good opportunity to talk about their fitness goals after things have settled down with their new-born.

Recognise that this is going to be a really new experience for your client. Her body, outlook and priorities have very likely changed. Be understanding of all of these factors and don't look to force her back into the gym, but do look to offer other services as a first step (such as providing detailed nutrition programmes and recommended exercises).

Many of the steps above take little effort but can make the key difference between "just another gym business" and a client-centred business that cares about the individual circumstances of its customers.

THE "WORK-A-HOLIC" CLIENT

Your goal is to be one of the best trainers in the business whose track record of success commands the highest hourly rates. Inevitably, therefore, your client list will contain some of the best, the brightest and most ambitious people around. The people who want it all from life...and then some! This has its downsides – stress, anxiety and tiredness tend to be common with this group.

These are the clients you definitely want on your books because they pay well and pay reliably, but you need to be aware of the characteristics that define these types of people so that you fit seamlessly into their life. I have worked with many so called "work-a-holic" clients – and, I confess that I became a work-a-holic myself for many years.

There is nothing wrong with someone who has a strong work ethic; you just need to spot the signs of someone who is simply pushing themselves far too hard for no reason. Ensure that the training programmes you deliver are really helping them and not creating unwelcome additional stress! Here are my guidelines to get the best out of this personality type:

Be tough but fair. They don't want their gym trainer to be a pushover. Be clear at the outset of your relationship that you have a rigorous, disciplined approach to your work and them keeping to the schedule. Schedule gym sessions for fixed dates and times.

Draw attention to your cancellation policy at the outset. Mine works like this: I operate a cancellation policy of at least 48 hours' notice. I make an exception where the client or their close family member appears to be genuinely very ill. Last minute "work commitments", however, are generally not a valid reason for cancelling a session. The way most private medical and dental services work is that specifying "work commitments" as the reason for cancellation does not entitle the patient to a refund. Why should the professional fitness industry be any different? My basic philosophy is that if the client is getting paid, then I am getting paid.

Payment – I would also suggest you set up a scheduled payment (such as a direct debit or standing order) with this type of client. As a commercially-minded, ambitious person who demands results and consistency, they will understand and appreciate this business-like approach.

Judgement – as a general matter, use your judgement. If you are a new business with a new, high profile, corporate client, taking a hard line towards cancellations at an early stage may backfire and damage relationships. You will know where to give people a little bit of flexibility and when to strictly enforce your cancellations policy. If you have established yourself as a trusted advisor to a "work-a-holic" client, do not be afraid to charge them for a missed session. If you're starting up and trying to establish a foothold in the corporate world, don't tarnish your relationship before it begins. A little bit of flexibility here and there can help immensely in fostering a good early relationship.

If time pressure appears to be a problem for your client, you may want to suggest a 30- or 45-minute session as standard as opposed to longer 1-hour sessions. 45 minutes is ample time to complete most exercise sessions!

Get up early! Typically, this type of client prefers to exercise in the early hours of the morning before heading to the office. Countless studies have shown that training in the morning will create a greater overall health benefit. There will be less chance of the client cancelling if you are the first item on their busy agenda. If you object to working long and unusual hours to accommodate your clients, you're almost certainly in the wrong industry. Until you've built a successful business you need to put the hours in. The world is more competitive than ever, and if you don't go the extra mile to work around your client's packed schedule, there are plenty of other more committed businesses that will – and ultimately you will lose out. Always remember: it's called work for a reason. You only need to look at the car your client drives to recognise that working long hours does pay off!

Recognise when your client is stressed. This means you should listen to them closely for any clues that they have a problem with work or balancing the endless demands of corporate and family life. Exercise is a form of stress: putting your client through a tough workout when they are, for example, already adrenally stressed is going to wipe them out even more. Educate them on the benefits of rest, relaxation and good nutrition as part of an overall approach to health to support their stressed state.

Go through a stretching session prior to or after the training session. Teach them relaxation techniques such as breathing exercises.

Give them a meditation audio recording.

This type of client will thrive on challenge – keep them interested with regular challenges and goals (with this type of client, "tough love" is a legitimate strategy – don't be afraid of damaging their ego; they appreciate the truth to help them produce results based on honest feedback – they are paying you to be tough on them).

Any person in business is driven by numbers. So set your goals with this client and then work out what numbers are most important to them. Is it the tape measure, scales, calliper readings or the weights on the end of that Olympic bar? (I am in favour of avoiding "vanity" in my workouts and focusing on the overall health and wellbeing of my clients rather than how wide their biceps are – but for some this is the most important metric!) Be sure to report these numbers to them each week to maintain momentum.

Learn from them. Learn from their good traits that have enabled them to become successful in business and learn from their mistakes in becoming addicted to the work that they do! Show interest in what they do and ask open-ended questions. When they tell you, for example, they are an accountant in the city, ask "How did you get into that?" They'll rejoice in telling you their life story and reveal valuable information about their character, their life and ambitions. In the corporate world ego often comes before money, so make sure you position yourself as a trusted advisor to your client, who is willing to listen to their life story and goals.

THE INJURED CLIENT

Inevitably, clients get injured from time to time. Hopefully it's not during a training session that you are running. If a client is injured, it presents a real opportunity to go the "extra mile" and build that relationship with your client when times are down.

I'm sure you've been injured in the past, and as someone who has had multiple surgeries for various sports injuries, I know there's no worse a feeling than being unable to do what you love. I have become a little depressed by being unable to compete or train, and unless you surround yourself with others who know what you're going through it is hard to get through it.

It is at this time with your clients that you can show real value. Here's what to do:

Call them to see how they are (again, a simple step, but one that most trainers do not take).

Work out what you can do to meaningfully help them. Platitudes like "get well soon" on their own will not work. On the other hand, maybe you can assist them yourself with a stretch session, a massage or corrective exercises?

Look at your list of useful contacts – is there anyone on the list that you think can specifically help them? Be the guy that "connects" people; you'll be valued by both parties!

Can you book the appointment for them or in any other way facilitate the appointment and make the appropriate introduction?

Can you contact the therapist before or after the treatment to gain a deeper understanding of your client's injury and determine how long they will be out of action for, or how you can adapt their training?

If the client needs several sessions with the therapist, can you build a relationship with that therapist? Not only will this benefit your client but it will make a huge impression on the therapist and potentially open up a new referral source.

Remember to call or text them each week at their training time.

If they need to stop training for a sustained period of time arrange to meet them for an informal coffee one week at their usual training time to have a chat, keep their spirits up and make plans for their future training – create the sense that you are working towards recovery with them as a team.

Find something else for them to do. For example, is there a hydrotherapy pool or isolation tank centre that could help nearby?

Pencil in a target date for their training to resume to keep them motivated and inspired.

THE CLIENT MOVES AWAY

Your financial goal should be to build multiple sources of income. Remember that it is always easier to sell to someone who has purchased from you before than sell to a completely new client or lead.

Simply keeping clients' details on file, adding them to your mailing list, inviting them to your communities and social media pages at an early stage allows you to contact them with "free" information that can provide them with real value and maintain your reputation.

If, for whatever reason, a client stops training with you, there is nothing to stop you from continuing to send them articles, workout videos, recipes, training ideas etc.

If you gain a client's trust over time through providing meaningful and useful content, it becomes easier to sell to them.

THE CLIENT GOES ON HOLIDAY

Before sending your client a killer workout to complete each day they're away you need to decide if they actually need to rest.

Are they burnt out?

Are they showing signs of adrenal exhaustion?

If so, leave them to it. Send them away with your best wishes, let them rest, recover and let their hair down. Just make sure you've booked them in for a session when they get back!

If they do want to train whilst they are away then have you created a holiday workout programme (such as a bodyweight exercise)?

Can you sell them a product to take away with them?

THE CLIENT WHO CAN NO LONGER AFFORD YOU

We've discussed the difference between a cost and an investment already. If you are delivering an excellent service and achieving some great results for your clients then your clients will see you as a great investment; a necessity in their lives and not a luxury spend that they can do without.

However, life can throw up all sorts of surprises: people lose jobs, relationships end and huge, unexpected bills arrive on doorsteps.

How your client reacts to these circumstances is out of your control. How YOU react to their decision could well give you an opportunity to make your relationship even stronger. Showing compassion and understanding for their situation at this time is your first priority. I've heard stories of trainers throwing tantrums and arguing with clients for being selfish because they have decided they can no longer afford to work with them.

Accept the client's situation and offer alternatives that are more cost efficient. Here are some ideas I have used in the past to good effect:

Can you reduce the number of times that you see them each week?

Can you actually empower them to train on their own and use you as their coach who writes their programmes, takes their measurements, charts their progress and just meets with them on a monthly basis to review everything?

Can you do 30-minute sessions?

Can you offer small group or class sessions for them?

Do you have an online programme to refer them to?

Can you tailor something really specific to their needs?

Capitalise on this opportunity to grow as a great, resourceful coach who understands and responds to the financial predicaments of your clients.

This book is all about building relationships with clients in order to keep them coming back to you, but you can't keep offering them the same old boring thing. The service you deliver needs to change in order to motivate them and to motivate YOU. This type of situation is a great opportunity for you to expand your horizons.

Being a personal trainer is a great career that anyone would love doing. However, delivering 30-40 minute, predictable one-to-one sessions week after week after week is not the goal. It's unsustainable and will cause you to grow bored and burnt out at some point, I can guarantee that!

Change is ALWAYS a good thing.

SOMETHING TO THINK ABOUT

To go alongside the other "special situations" in this chapter, from time to time you'll encounter a critical problem with clients that may be difficult to fix: they simply don't like you!

Most people don't want to tell you the cold, hard truth and so they will find a reasonable excuse that has the desired effect without causing too much upset. We've all heard this before:

"It's not you, it's me."

It's an easy way out for clients who simply don't want to work with you anymore. So before you start looking into alternative options you can offer your client, have a good look at the current service you have been providing. Think about the following:

If you see a client at the end of a 15-hour day when things haven't quite gone to plan, what kind of training session are they going to get?

If you see that client every week at the end of a 15-hour day, what kind of experience are they going to have with you?

If you bitch and moan to them for an hour will they want to continue working with you?

If you just go through the motions, shouting numbers at them week after week, do you really think they will want to keep working with you?

The words 'I can't afford you' could quite easily be code for 'I cannot stand to work with you any longer and I resent handing over my hard-earned cash to a tired, miserable, uninterested trainer!'

Change yourself first then look at what you can change for your clients.

CHAPTER 24
IN SUMMARY

BASIC TIPS FOR INSTANT SUCCESS IN THIS BUSINESS

IF YOU WANT to become a Trusted Trainer, stick to these golden rules and you will succeed where hordes of other personal training businesses fail:

- Always be punctual.
- Always say 'thank you' – it goes a very long way!
- Always deliver a well thought out, client-centred, personalised session for your client (see the above sections of this book).
- When interacting with clients, always be "present in the moment", engaged and maintaining good eye contact (even if you have many other distractions the client comes first).
- Always return a call promptly.
- Always acknowledge emails and text messages very promptly to confirm you have safely received them; a reply in full can come later but the client will get the sense that you are responsive if you send a one line "holding email" shortly after receipt.
- The big one: if you say you'll do something, make sure you do it. People judge your integrity by this and "letting things slide" if you're "too busy" never flies in business.

No matter how basic these things may seem, if you do them consistently then people will trust you. They will want to help you. They will know you are a dependable person and will want to spend time with, and money on, you.

THE PRINCIPLES OF SUCCESS
PLAN

The key to any successful business is to plan well in advance. Make sure you are always planning ahead. Once you've mapped out your week, the things you need to do, the people you need to speak to and the resources you'll need for each task, you've already gained the upper hand against your competitors and your clients. Keep a "to-do" list and cross items off as you complete tasks during the week, giving you peace of mind that you have done everything you needed to come Friday night!

If you don't plan your week, other people will shoehorn themselves into your schedule, which will ultimately be a drain on your time. Remember what I said earlier about creating recurring time slots in your diary for each client? Not only does it work well for them but it gives you a clear routine to follow. Make sure you also book regular times for:

- your own training;
- your business admin;
- writing up client fitness programmes;
- contacting clients on a formal or informal basis (depending on how well you know them!);
- for your own continued education and development; and most importantly time away from work!

Do this and you will always own your business, rather than it owning YOU!

It's great to have the freedom to take time out in the middle of the day to train and to have the ability to move appointments around as you see fit, but if you really want to move forward with your business you need to create time to work ON your business as well as IN your business. You may be spending a lot of time helping clients push out that last vital rep but how much time do you spend brainstorming and strategizing to make sure you out-think your competition in business? I'm willing to bet not enough!

PLAN YOUR WEEK

If you have a free schedule how do you know what you should be working on each week?

Know how each day looks and, if possible, what each hour of each day of the week looks like. My advice is to take time at the start of each day to decide what you want to happen and review this at the end of each day. Never be surprised, however, when an unexpected event that must be prioritised puts paid to all of your plans for the day or week.

Tackle the hardest or most tedious things first while your willpower is at its highest. If there's a bill that needs paying or your tax return is late, focus on those items first rather than designing your next "ground-breaking fitness innovation" that you insist will make you millions.

Just as you track your client's progress, you need to take the time to track your own progress on a day-to-day basis. Here's how I do it:

START OF THE DAY QUESTIONS

What one thing can I do today to take my business and my life forwards?
What things would I do today to make it an AMAZING day?

END OF THE DAY QUESTIONS

How would I rate my day out of ten? What could be improved tomorrow?

If you really want to succeed with your business then you should have a clear vision of what your business is going to look like in the future. Just remember that it is YOUR business, so ignore what others are doing, block out the noise of social media and the distractions of those who are jealous of your ambition and follow your own path to excellence. Very often you'll find that turning to "experts" for "advice" does not produce results. Only YOU know the true destiny of your business and the heights you are capable of achieving. The path to success is a continuous process of surpassing your previous best, and a difficult path that very few will ever choose to take. It's not all glory; far from it. You have to push that boulder up the hill every day, every week, every year; but if you knuckle down with the nitty gritty, you'll have moved a mountain ten years down the road.

BE PASSIONATE

Here's a final thought for you to reflect on in order to ensure that you make a success of your personal training business.

ALWAYS do what you love and love what you do.

Hopefully you've chosen to work in this industry because you're genuinely passionate about health and fitness for yourself and because you want to help others to change their lives.

When you follow your passion, the hours of tedium and drudge work all become worth it. If you are really following your heart then you don't need to think too much about anything, you don't need to drag yourself out of bed, you don't complain about burning the midnight oil or working over the weekend because you love it. When you are in this state you are full of energy, you feel as though you can keep going forever, you have a smile on your face and everything is good with the world. This is called a flow state in psychology (look it up if you want to learn more). I've worked with many accountants, lawyers and doctors who have totally lost the passion in their lives – don't be that guy!

The act of running your own business means that, inevitably, you will have to do some jobs that bore you. Your bills need paying, your tax return is not done, your rented space has a leaky roof, a difficult client is complaining; the list goes on. The thought of going into work early to do the end of month reports probably isn't going to get your juices flowing but it's a necessity when running a business; without them you'll go under. Until such time as you have enough money to employ someone to do the tedious work, embrace it – it is all worth it because you are running a business that you care passionately about – that is much more than most accountants, doctors or lawyers can honestly say! If you embrace these tasks, you increase your own value as a person because by definition, these are the difficult, grubby tasks that most mediocre people shy away from.

Make some big decisions NOW and remain passionate about your work. Learn from my mistakes and don't spend a second more of your time doing any of these things:

- Don't spend time with clients that you are not passionate about working with.
- Don't spend time with other trainers you don't want to work with.
- Don't carry on doing something that doesn't excite you anymore; cut your losses and move on.

I mentioned right at the beginning of this book that if you are about to start a training business, you are at a critical stage in your life. You are making the transition from trainer to business owner. If you want to spend all of your time working with clients then you are not behaving like a business owner, you are behaving like an employee. Save your "gym floor time" for your premium clients who are key to your business as and where necessary. Delegate work where you can so you can focus on the bigger picture. Always be an owner; never be a minion.

The workout principles in my gym are based on the fundamental principles that underpin my personal training method. Despite that, my time is far better spent making the big day-to-day business decisions, thinking strategically about the business going forward and addressing significant problems. I have a team of people who follow my method and where necessary I can step into the cut and thrust of the gym floor, but it's not my preference and it's not healthy for my business.

One should always embrace change. Spending your life doing the same thing day in, day out is a colossal waste of your time. It may be difficult to move on but if you're not growing anywhere, then you're not going anywhere.

I am still incredibly passionate about my business and work on the gym floor; I continue to consult with a small number of key clients. I just get more of a buzz from managing a team of great people who implement my method for me and from creating new opportunities for business expansion.

DO GREAT WORK

As Steve Jobs famously said: *'the only way to do great work is to love what you do. So keep finding those new things that you love, keep challenging yourself and always be passionate about every aspect of your work.'*

I believe that life is all about chasing your dreams whatever your ambitions, big or small. What would your life be like if it was absolutely amazing? Write it down now in glorious detail. Once you've established that, you'll have a better sense of how to act and which decisions to take in the humdrum and grind of daily entrepreneurial life.

'Never settle' (another gem from the late Steve Jobs). Imagine that perfect life that just seems so far out of reach right now but something that you can fix your mind on day after day and then pursue it with rigour, no matter what it takes. It may be a business idea, an adventure or a girl or guy you want to be with. If it is really your dream to have these things then with dedicated resolve, you will achieve it!

Obviously life changes and as a result, your dreams will need to be amended; you just need to keep pursuing the next dream with the same enthusiasm. Treat everything like your first project. You'll only be happy when you have a project to work on and a goal in mind that you are continually moving closer towards. The feeling of success at the top of the mountain is typically fleeting – so keep climbing.

I now have my dream business. The dream that I visualised a decade ago has been achieved and a lot more besides. I'm now moving onto a new set of dreams. This is one of them: to help others succeed through relaying my own experiences in the health and fitness industry.

Chase your dreams and don't let anyone or anything get in your way.

BE YOUR OWN BOSS

For years, I have battled with what I SHOULD do instead of what I really WANT to do. It's easy to get caught up in a world where we give so much to others that we either forget or simply no longer know how to give much to ourselves.

Great things really started happening for me as soon as I decided to put myself first. I know what you might say: I've got a wife, kids, a mortgage, I can't put myself first, I have responsibilities and I need to put the needs of others first. Bullshit! Stop telling yourself that story. Don't you think you'll be a better husband, a better father and be able to pay off the mortgage a lot more easily if you're doing what you genuinely love every day?

If you have a dream then please don't give up on it! Too many people give up on theirs at a young age and then they feel the need to talk others out of following theirs. Don't listen to them, don't follow the crowd, don't "get a proper job" or "do the right thing", don't join the rat race, don't settle for ordinary.

Keep dreaming, keep believing and keep going. It WILL be worth it.

CHAPTER 25
MY STORY

So here's my story, my journey so far,
On how I've become a fitness superstar.
I'll lay it all down, my hopes and fears,
and my adventures in the industry for the last 10 years.

With my degree in Sports Science I headed for the city,
I had the charm and good looks and my chat was quite witty.
The big box gyms were where I honed my skills,
But I had to go it alone to really pay the bills.

I got tired of the "normal life", it really made me yawn,
So without a second thought my first business was born.
A place of my own in exclusive Highgate,
I knew I'd change the world and tell it to them straight.

I got really busy and so my team grew,
A few more trainers and some therapists too.
I became a bit famous – a local fitness giant.
And started to work with "The Celebrity Client."

An investor came in and sold me the dream,
But all too quickly it came apart at the seams.
It was no longer my business and I was in a hole.
I'd jumped in without thinking and sold my soul!

I bought myself out and nearly lost it all,
But this wouldn't be a good story without the rise and fall!
I questioned my decisions and felt pretty rotten,
The dream became a nightmare and I hit rock bottom.

But life is a journey; you've got to play the games,
I rose from the ashes like a phoenix from the flames!
What doesn't kill you makes you stronger, or so the saying goes,
Now I focus on the good stuff and learn from the lows.

I've had a second chance to re-build my dream,
With a different outlook and a powerful team.
I've started to run my business from afar,
And live my life like a superstar!

I've changed my habits to be smart and wise,
And within two years I've made it four times the size.
I've learned to love life and live without fear,
And leave my old ways to begin a new career.

I'm proud of what I've done, but I need to move on,
It's all about the future, what's in the past has gone.
Building my gym in London has been just fine,
But exciting new adventures are waiting to be mine…

CHAPTER 26
HOW TO WORK WITH DAVID - TRAINING PROGRAMMES AND CONSULTATIONS

IF YOU'VE ENJOYED the ideas set out in this book, there are a number of ways you can seek advice and assistance from David directly, either in person at your business premises or at David's state-of-the-art fitness studios in North London. Consultations and personal business coaching sessions with David are also available by Skype, email and telephone. If you'd like to find out more about any of the following courses please contact David's team on:

consultations@davidosgathorp.com
Or visit: http://davidosgathorp.com/doconsultancy

OPTION 1: HOW TO SET UP YOUR OWN PERSONAL TRAINING STUDIO (INTENSIVE WEEKEND BUSINESS BOOTCAMP)

Join David in person for an intensive business workshop over the course of a full weekend at his state-of-the-art fitness studios in Highgate, North London. The agenda is packed and you'll learn:

- How to build a personal training business from zero to 1000 one-to-one personal training sessions per month
- How to stand out from the hordes of other hopeful trainers in this saturated marketplace
- How to find your unique selling point in the fitness industry
- How to partner with other businesses to grow your brand
- How to build incredible relationships with key clients for life
- How to build an award-winning team
- Why you should never just rent space in your studio
- Why you must never settle for anything less than excellence
- Why you should continually aim to progress and insist that those junior to you take on more responsibility so you can focus on the big important business decisions, avoiding the trap of micro-managing.

By the end of this weekend workshop you'll leave with a tailored plan of action to take your business to the next level.

OPTION 2: ONE DAY BUSINESS MAKEOVER

In just one (very long) day, you'll be given a complete plan of action to turbo-charge your business and, more importantly, improve your life.

Before working with David you'll be sent a pre-consultation questionnaire to determine the present strengths and weaknesses of your fitness business. David will conduct a detailed review of this self-completed report and identify areas for improvement. You will then be invited to join David for a 60-minute phone consultation (at a date and time prior to the meeting in person) so that you know what to expect from the session and David fully understands the circumstances of your business and the stage that it is at.

The Format of the Day:

- Early breakfast meeting: outlining the plan for the day and the primary objectives
- Goal-setting for yourself and your business
- Marketing Plan
- Customer Service Plan
- SWOT Analysis
- Studio Makeover
- Marketing Materials Makeover
- Client Generation
- Operations Manual

By the end of the day your business will look better, work better, generate more leads and more importantly ignite the passion within you to enjoy taking your business and your life to a new level.

OPTION 3: TWELVE WEEK MENTORING PROGRAMME

If you are running a coaching business then I have found there is always value in having a coach *yourself* to provide feedback and to motivate you when necessary. Ideally this would be someone with more experience than you in the same industry. David is ideally placed (with 20 years of experience) to offer this 12-week mentoring service to beginner, intermediate and upper-intermediate trainers. This programme will take you from a great coach to a great leader and business person.

The aim of the coaching sessions is to determine where your passion lies and build a plan around working only in your passion. For example, in my experience, many trainers actually have different aims and life goals:

- If you want to be the best coach and work with great clients for the next ten years we will focus on the mechanics of personal training and less on the business and finance side.
- If you're an ambitious entrepreneurial business owner with big ambitions to eventually own a large business and would like to expand rapidly, we will discuss in detail the key challenges involved and how to overcome them!
- If your goal is to build a business that works without you being present and generates "passive income", then we will work together to realign your business model for this purpose.

Whatever your goal, you will have full access to my business advice, my contacts and my guidance to get you to up the learning curve fast – an unfair advantage over all other trainers starting from scratch.

- You will be personally invited to my studios in Highgate, North London, for a one-on-one meeting and to see how my business runs on a day-to-day basis.

You will be taken through a step-by-step process that will enable you to:

- Define the values for yourself and your business
- Determine your WHY
- Create your unique definition of "excellence"
- Determine your "ideal client"
- Build your unique brand
- Create your unique message
- Build your own team
- Critique, refine and design your new marketing materials
- Determine your daily and weekly goals for the next 12 weeks
- Determine your weekly, monthly and quarterly goals for the next 12 months.

Your business will look better, function in a better way and give you a far better income. The coaching sessions will allow us to analyse every aspect of your business, focus on the key aspects that are working, improve the areas that are causing you problems and remove the things that are letting you down.

In just twelve weeks from now, you will be clear on exactly what you do, how you do it and most importantly, WHY you do it.

For more information on these courses (including pricing information) please visit: http://davidosgathorp.com/doconsultancy

ABOUT THE AUTHOR

DAVID FOUNDED HIS company, All About You, in 2006 with a credit card and a real belief in his own ability. Within a few years he had grown it to a multiple six-figure business and had numerous offers of investment in his brand. Over the last ten years, he has remained at the forefront of the health and fitness industry and has had the opportunity to work personally with numerous celebrities, professional athletes and successful entrepreneurs.

David's own entrepreneurial career has included starting, building, financing, partnering and selling businesses. He is now an award-winning business owner and regarded as a leader in the health and fitness industry.

He currently spends his time working with his award-winning team, writing for his own in-house publications and for numerous industry and consumer publications. He still coaches a number of celebrity clients and also works each week in his dream role as health and wellbeing consultant to Red Bull Racing Formula One Team.

Away from work he plays the guitar and is also currently pursuing another lifelong ambition of gaining his private pilot's licence.

Printed in Great Britain
by Amazon